weightwatchers

THE LITTLE BIG BOOK OF FRUITS & VEGGIES

Weight Watchers Publishing Group

VP Content/Editor in Chief **Theresa DiMasi**

Creative Director **Ed Melnitsky**

Associate Editor **Katerina Gkionis**

Food Editor **Eileen Runyan**

Writer and Project Editor **Alice K. Thompson**

Contributing Editor **Lisa Chernick**

Contributing Editor **Leslie Fink, MS, RD**

Photo Director **Marybeth Dulany**

Nutrition Consultant **Linda Wang**

Production Manager **Alan Biederman**

Art Director **Daniela A. Hriṭcu**

Art/Production Assistant **Rebecca Kollmer**

Photographer **Christopher Testani**

Food Stylist **Chris Lanier**

Prop Stylist **Carla Gonzalez-Hart**

SKU #11967

Printed in the USA

Front cover:
Lemony Sugar Snap Pea Salad, page 222

Back cover:
Orange Salad with Mint and Orange Flower Water, page 117

ABOUT WEIGHT WATCHERS INTERNATIONAL, INC.

Weight Watchers International, Inc. is the world's leading commercial provider of weight-management services, operating globally through a network of company-owned and franchise operations. Weight Watchers holds more than 36,000 meetings each week at which members receive group support and learn about healthy eating patterns, behavior modification, and physical activity. Weight Watchers provides innovative digital weight management products through its websites, mobile sites, and apps. Weight Watchers is the leading provider of online subscription weight management products in the world. In addition, Weight Watchers offers a wide range of products, publications, and programs for those interested in weight loss and weight control.

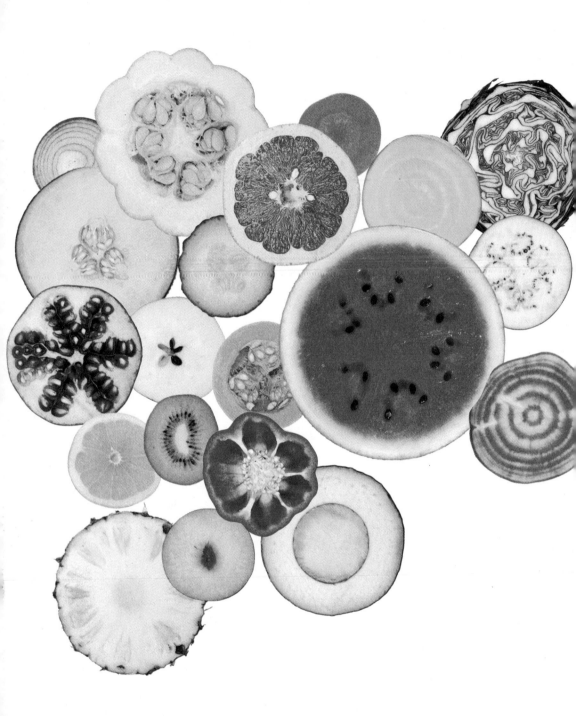

CONTENTS

ABOUT OUR RECIPES

While losing weight isn't only about what you eat, Weight Watchers realizes the critical role it plays in your success and overall good health. That's why our philosophy is to offer great-tasting, easy recipes that are nutritious as well as delicious. We create most of our recipes with the healthy and filling foods we love: lots of fresh fruits and vegetables, most of which have 0 SmartPoints value, and with satisfying lean proteins, which are low in SmartPoints. We also try to ensure that our recipes fall within the recommendations of the U.S. Dietary Guidelines for Americans so that they support a diet that promotes health and reduces the risk for disease. If you have special dietary needs, consult with your health-care professional for advice on a diet that is best for you, then adapt these recipes to meet your specific nutritional needs.

Get started, keep going, and enjoy good nutrition

At Weight Watchers, we believe that eating well makes life better, no matter where you are in your weight-loss journey. These delicious recipes are ideal, whether you're just getting started or have already reached your goals on the SmartPoints plan. Unlike other weight-loss programs, which focus solely on calories, the SmartPoints plan guides you toward healthier foods that are lower in sugar and saturated fat, and higher in protein. But this isn't a diet—all food is "in." Eating well should be fun, energizing, and delicious, so that healthy food choices become second nature. To get maximum satisfaction, we suggest that you keep the following information in mind while preparing our recipes.

➻ SmartPoints values are given for each recipe. The SmartPoints for each ingredient is assigned based on the number of calories and amount of saturated fat, sugar, and protein per the ingredient quantity. The SmartPoints for each ingredient are then added together and divided by the number of servings, and the result is rounded.

➻ Recipes include approximate nutritional information: They are analyzed for Calories (Cal), Total Fat, Saturated Fat (Sat Fat), Sodium (Sod), Total Carbohydrates (Total Carb), Sugar, Dietary Fiber (Fib), and Protein (Prot). The nutritional values are obtained from the Weight Watchers database, which is maintained by registered dietitians.

➻ Substitutions made to the ingredients could alter the per-serving nutritional information and may affect the SmartPoints.

➻ To boost flavor, we often include fresh herbs or a squeeze of citrus instead of increasing the salt. If you don't have to restrict your sodium intake, feel free to add a touch more salt as desired.

➤ Recipes in this book that are designated gluten free do not contain any wheat (in all forms, including kamut, semolina, spelt, and triticale), barley, or rye, as well as products that are made from these ingredients, such as breads, couscous, pastas, seitan, soy sauce, beer, malt vinegar, and malt beverages. Other foods such as salad dressings, Asian-style sauces, salsa and tomato sauce, shredded cheese, yogurt, and sour cream may be sources of gluten. Check ingredient labels carefully on packaged foods that we call for, as different brands of the same premade food product may or may not contain gluten. If you are following a gluten-free diet because you have celiac disease, please consult your health-care professional.

➤ Cook's Tip suggestions have a SmartPoints value of 0 unless otherwise stated.

➤ For information about the science behind lasting weight loss and more, please visit WeightWatchers.com/science.

Calculations not what you expected?

SmartPoints for the recipes in this book are calculated without counting any fruits and most vegetables, but the nutrition information does include the nutrient content from fruits and vegetables. This means you may get a different SmartPoints value if you calculate the SmartPoints based on the nutrition. To allow for your "free" fruits and veggies, use the SmartPoints assigned to the recipes. Also, please note, when fruits and veggies are liquefied or pureed (as in a smoothie), their nutrient content is incorporated into the recipe calculations. These nutrients can increase the SmartPoints.

Alcohol is included in our SmartPoints calculations. Because alcohol information is generally not included on nutrition labels, it's not an option you can include when using the handlheld or online calculator or in the Weight Watchers app. But since we include the alcohol information that we get from our database in our recipes, you might notice discrepancies between the SmartPoints you see here in our recipes, and the values you get using the calculator. The SmartPoints listed for our recipes are the most accurate values.

Simply Filling (the no-count option)

If counting SmartPoints isn't your thing, try Simply Filling, a no-count technique. To follow it, eat just until satisfied, primarily from the list of Simply Filling foods found in your *Pocket Guide*. For more information, see your member guidebook.

Choosing ingredients

As you learn to eat healthier and add more wholesome foods to your meals, consider the following to help you choose foods wisely:

LEAN MEATS AND POULTRY
Purchase lean meats and poultry, and trim them of all visible fat before cooking. When poultry is cooked with the skin on, we recommend removing the skin before eating. Nutritional information for recipes that include meat, poultry, and fish is based on cooked, skinless boneless portions (unless otherwise stated), with the fat trimmed.

SEAFOOD
Whenever possible, our recipes call for seafood that is sustainable and deemed the most healthful for human consumption so that your choice of seafood is not only good for the oceans but also

good for you. For more information about the best seafood choices and to download a pocket guide, go to the Environmental Defense Fund at seafood.edf.org or seafoodwatch.org.

PRODUCE

For best flavor, maximum nutrient content, and the lowest prices, buy fresh local produce, such as vegetables, leafy greens, and fruits in season. Rinse them thoroughly before using, and keep a supply of cut-up vegetables and fruits in your refrigerator for convenient healthy snacks.

WHOLE GRAINS

Explore your market for whole-grain products such as whole wheat and whole-grain breads and pastas, brown rice, bulgur, barley, cornmeal, whole wheat couscous, oats, and quinoa to enjoy with your meals.

Read the recipe

Take a couple of minutes to read through the ingredients and directions before you start to prepare a recipe. This will prevent you from discovering midway through that you don't have an important ingredient or that a recipe requires several hours of marinating. And it's also a good idea to assemble all ingredients and utensils within easy reach before you begin cooking.

Weighing and measuring

The success of any recipe depends on accurate weighing and measuring. The effectiveness of the Weight Watchers Program and the accuracy of the nutritional analysis depend on correct measuring as well. Use the following techniques:

Weigh foods such as meat, poultry, and fish on a food scale.

To measure liquids, use a standard glass or plastic measuring cup placed on a level surface. For amounts less than ¼ cup, use standard measuring spoons.

To measure dry ingredients, use metal or plastic measuring cups that come in ¼-, ⅓-, ½-, and 1-cup sizes. Fill the appropriate cup, and level it with the flat edge of a knife or spatula. For amounts less than ¼ cup, use standard measuring spoons.

PRODUCE PRIMER

Fresh produce—it's delicious, it's beautiful, and its year-round variety is an inspiration in the kitchen as well as a connection to the changing seasons. We already know that fruits and vegetables are good for us, but now there's another big reason to love them: Almost all of them have zero SmartPoints.

There are a few exceptions. Of the produce items covered in this book, avocados, corn, green peas, parsnips, and potatoes do have SmartPoints values. And any fruit or vegetable that is pureed for drinking—such as in a smoothie or in a juice preparation—should be counted toward your daily SmartPoints Target.

So dive in and get all the practical knowledge and expert tips you need to enjoy 56 of the most popular fruits and vegetables, from apples to zucchini. Then turn to "Our Freshest Recipes," starting on page 71, for easy ways to put these favorites to work.

Happy eating!

Theresa DiMasi
VP Content/Editor in Chief

FRUITS

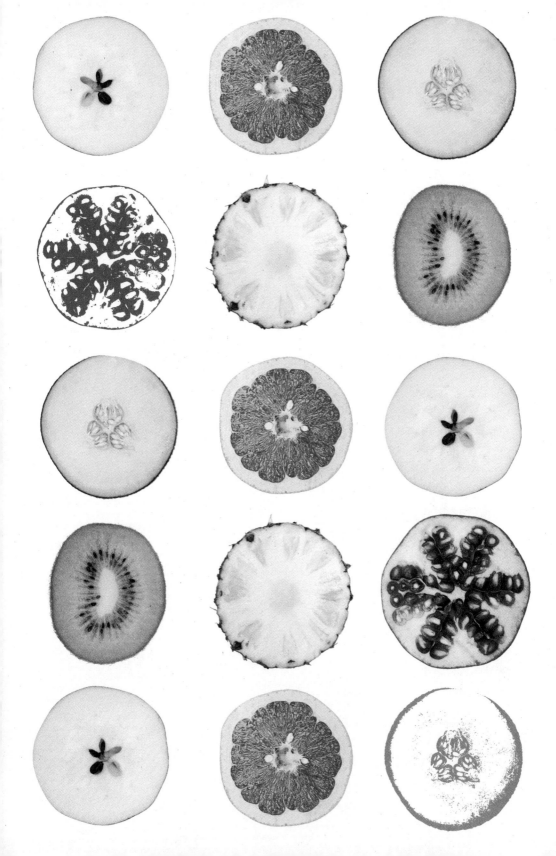

APPLES

While there are thousands of apple varieties grown worldwide, you're probably familiar with only a handful. The types available at supermarkets tend to be those that travel and store well rather than taste exceptional. Visit orchards and markets during apple season, and you'll discover lesser-known, heirloom, and local varieties, a revelation in deliciousness.

IN SEASON
September to December

➠CHOOSING & STORING
• Look for apples with glossy, firm, unblemished skin. Apples should have a fresh, lightly floral fragrance; pass on any that smell musty or sour.
• One bad apple spoils the bunch: Here's an old wives' tale that's actually true. Damaged or overripe apples produce higher levels of ethylene, a compound that stimulates the fruit around it to ripen faster, so remove any damaged apples immediately.
• Keep apples in a cool area of your kitchen if you plan to use them within a few days. For longer storage, place them in a sealed plastic bag and refrigerate them up to several weeks.
• Stop cut apples from browning by brushing them with lemon or orange juice, or keep them in a bowl of acidulated water—water to which you've added the juice of half a lemon.
• Consider buying organic; conventionally grown apples have one of the highest levels of pesticide residue of any fruit.

➠USE 'EM UP!
• Grate apples and add them to muffins, meat loaf, soups, salads, sandwiches, slaws, and more; they can add moisture, natural sweetness, extra fiber, and nutrition to hundreds of dishes.
• Slice apples and layer them in sandwiches; they have a natural affinity for cheese, ham, turkey, and nut butters.
• Pair apples with sage, rosemary, thyme, caraway, or coriander in savory dishes; team them with cinnamon, cloves, ginger, nutmeg, star anise, or vanilla in both sweet and savory dishes.
• Mix apples with other fruits in sauces, salads, and desserts; they're excellent with berries, cranberries, figs, oranges, pears, and pomegranates.

➠GOOD FOR YOU
Apples are an excellent source of fiber and vitamin C, and contain high amounts of the antioxidant quercetin. Almost half of an apple's vitamin C and most of its fiber are found in its skin, so eat them unpeeled for maximum nutritional benefit. Because pesticides are also concentrated in the skin, always scrub nonorganic apples gently under cold running water before eating.

braeburn

Crisp, firm, lightly tart and refreshing

BEST FOR:
Eating, applesauce, pie

GOOD TO KNOW:
Stores well, making it a good choice outside of apple season

empire

Crisp, juicy, sweet-tart

BEST FOR:
Eating, salads

GOOD TO KNOW:
Resists browning better than most varieties

honeycrisp

Very crisp, juicy, sweet

BEST FOR:
Eating, salads, cooking, baking

GOOD TO KNOW:
Outstanding for eating raw

cortland

Crisp, juicy, tangy, fragrant

BEST FOR: Eating, stewing, applesauce, pie

GOOD TO KNOW:
Resists browning better than most varieties

crispin

Crisp, explosively juicy, sweet

BEST FOR:
Eating, applesauce, baking

GOOD TO KNOW:
Sometimes known as Matsu

granny smith

Very firm and crisp, tart to very tart

BEST FOR:
Eating, slicing for sandwiches and salads, baking, applesauce, pie

GOOD TO KNOW:
A top all-purpose apple; stores well, making it a good choice outside of apple season. Resists browning.

jonathan

Juicy, sweet-tart, spicy

BEST FOR:
Eating, salads, applesauce, pie

GOOD TO KNOW:
Quality is variable, so it's worth sampling one before buying a lot

gravenstein

Crisp, juicy, lightly tart

BEST FOR:
Pie, sauce, baking

GOOD TO KNOW:
An early-season apple, outstanding for pie. Stores poorly, so not recommended after September

gala

Crisp, juicy, sweet, fragrant, lightly spicy

BEST FOR:
Eating, salads, cooking, applesauce

GOOD TO KNOW:
Complex flavor makes this tops for eating raw

fuji

Very crunchy, juicy, very sweet

BEST FOR:
Eating, baking whole

GOOD TO KNOW:
Stores well, making it a good choice outside of apple season

jonagold

Crisp, sweet-tart

BEST FOR:
Eating, applesauce, baking

GOOD TO KNOW:
A cross between Jonathan and Golden Delicious

macintosh

Tender, juicy, sweet-tart

BEST FOR:
Eating, salads, applesauce

GOOD TO KNOW:
Cooks down very quickly; good for sauce but not for baking

red delicious

Juicy, sweet

BEST FOR:
Eating, salads

GOOD TO KNOW:
Stores well, but can become mealy

lady

Very small, crisp, sweet-tart

BEST FOR:
Garnishing, eating, baking

GOOD TO KNOW:
Attractive minis; classic for garnishing platters and surrounding holiday roasts

golden delicious

Juicy, very sweet, lightly honey-flavored

BEST FOR:
Eating, cooking, applesauce, pie, baking

GOOD TO KNOW:
Choose carefully; can become mealy and bland with age

rome

Crisp, firm, sweet-tart

BEST FOR:
Baking, applesauce

GOOD TO KNOW:
Outstanding for baking whole

BANANAS

Although hundreds of banana varieties are grown worldwide, the slender yellow Cavendish banana is by far the most widely available in the United States. If you can find them, dwarf (a.k.a. finger) bananas are a real treat: These miniatures are supersweet, with a flavor that's slightly more floral than that of regular bananas. Less common are red bananas, which turn purple when ripe, and have creamy, pink-tinged flesh.

⇥ CHOOSING & STORING

Bananas are one of the few fruits that ripen better in your kitchen than they do on the plant, and that's good news because the majority of bananas in our markets are grown in South or Central America and shipped green to the United States. It also means there's little guesswork involved when it comes to picking out a good bunch: Just look for smooth, unblemished skins that have few (if any) brown spots and allow the fruit to ripen at room temperature.

• Speed up the ripening process by storing bananas in a paper bag with an apple.

• Refrigeration will permanently halt the ripening process, so refrigerate bananas only if they have reached ideal sweetness; the skins will continue to darken but the flesh will remain unchanged.

⇥ USE 'EM UP!

• Almost everyone has an opinion when it comes to how ripe the ideal banana should be. Some prefer the firmer, mildly flavored fruit whose green skin is barely tinged with yellow, while others crave the sweeter, softer flesh of a yellow fruit spotted with black. Personal preference aside, there are a few rules of thumb for using bananas in recipes:

Cooking or roasting whole: Greener, firmer, less-ripe bananas are preferable because they'll hold their shape better.

Slicing and eating raw or frozen: Bright yellow, medium-ripe fruit that's sweet but still not mushy.

Mashing and baking: Very ripe fruit that's spotted with brown will have the fullest flavor, making it ideal for recipes like banana bread.

• Faced with a glut of over-ripening bananas? Freeze them! Peel, slice, wrap well in plastic, and freeze up to 6 months. They can even go right from the freezer into the blender for smoothies.

• Stirring mashed bananas into the batter of baked goods adds terrific flavor, natural sweetness, and moisture. Try replacing up to half the butter or oil in breads or cookies with banana.

⇥ GOOD FOR YOU

A medium banana delivers a whopping amount (more than 400 mg) of potassium, an essential electrolyte.

BLACKBERRIES

Until recently these delicious berries had the reputation of being too sour for snacking and too thorny for cultivation. But thanks to the discovery of their antioxidant bonanza, plus the development of thornless bushes, blackberries are now more readily available and more popular than ever.

↪ CHOOSING & STORING

• Look for plump berries, and beware those that have stems attached: They may have been picked too early and may not ripen properly.
• Softness rather than color is the best indication of blackberry ripeness.
• Refrigerate berries for as short a time as possible. They lose flavor rapidly once harvested, and can go from ripe and wonderful to mushy and moldy in 1 or 2 days.
• Freeze blackberries if you're lucky enough to have a surplus. Place them in a single layer on a parchment-lined baking sheet and pop into the freezer until solid, 1 to 2 hours. Then transfer them to a zip-close plastic freezer bag and freeze up to 6 months.
• Blackberries are one of the fruits with the most residual pesticides, so consider buying organic if possible.

↪ USE 'EM UP!

• Blackberries' sweet-tart flavor make them a wonderful accompaniment to poultry, pork, or game. They can be roasted or cooked down in a pan sauce, or used as a raw garnish on the finished dish.
• Blackberries are excellent when mixed with sweeter fruits like pears, apples, melons, and strawberries.
• You can substitute blackberries in almost any recipe calling for raspberries. They're usually tangier than their red cousins, so adjust sugar or other flavorings accordingly.
• Turn a glass of sparkling water into a nonalcoholic cocktail by adding a few blackberries and a small sprig of mint or basil.

↪ GOOD FOR YOU

High fiber and a big dose of antioxidants make blackberries an ideal choice for snacking, cooking, and baking.

BLUEBERRIES

These powerful little berries are packed with so much good stuff that they've been referred to as "brain berries" and "youth berries." And with a sweet-tart balance that rivals any other berry, plus virtually no seeds, blueberries come pretty close to being the perfect fruit. Almost all the blueberries sold fresh in the United States are known as cultivated, or highbush, berries. The smaller wild, or lowbush, berries are usually sold frozen and are milder in flavor.

IN SEASON
April to September

➤ CHOOSING & STORING

• Look for plump, firm berries covered with the dusty, silvery bloom that's a sign of freshness.
• Buy only berries that are blue-black or deep indigo or purple; redness is a sign that the berries have been picked too early.
• Blueberries are usually sold in baskets or plastic clamshells. If you can, it's worthwhile to check that squished, moldy, or wrinkly berries haven't been hidden near the bottom.
• Refrigerate berries, loosely covered, for a few days; remove any that show signs of mold.
• Blueberries are one of the easiest berries to freeze. Just place unwashed berries loosely in an airtight container and freeze up to 6 months.

➤ USE 'EM UP!

• Blueberries are just as delicious in savory dishes as they are in sweet ones. Their flavor pairs particularly well with cinnamon, ginger, lemon, thyme, shallots, almonds, yogurt, and soft cheeses.
• Substitute frozen blueberries if fresh are out of season; the texture of frozen berries is a little mushy, but the flavor is excellent. If using in pancakes or muffins, add them in their frozen state to prevent their juices from bleeding into the batter.
• Add a few handfuls of fresh blueberries to your next salad, or blend fresh or frozen berries with a little vinegar, shallot, salt, and pepper for an excellent fat-free dressing.
• Rub your hands with lemon juice to help remove blueberry stains.

➤ GOOD FOR YOU

Because of their outstanding antioxidant content, blueberries may have a positive impact on risk factors for cardiovascular disease. Studies on animals have also shown that blueberries may help lower the risk of cancer and improve brain function, but more research is needed on humans. Wild blueberries are slightly higher in antioxidants than cultivated berries.

CANTALOUPE & HONEYDEW

Sweet, juicy, and divinely aromatic—nothing beats a perfectly ripe cantaloupe or honeydew for sheer fruit enjoyment. Dive into a melon half with a spoon, cut it into wedges, or pair its luscious flavor with other ingredients. Cantaloupe and honeydew are the most ubiquitous members of the muskmelon family, but look for galia, canary, and Crenshaw melons as well.

⤙ CHOOSING & STORING

Selecting and storing a melon for peak flavor takes a little knowledge; melons harvested too early will never reach their potential.

• For cantaloupes, look for pronounced netting on the skin with a background color of beige to golden and little or no green. Honeydews should have smooth, unblemished skin.

• Check that no stem is still attached to the melon; properly ripened melons "slip" from the vine, leaving only a slight indentation where they were attached. Also check that there is no bruising or mold here, a sign that the melon may already be too ripe.

• Finally, give the dimpled blossom end a sniff. A good melon should smell floral and slightly musky. If you smell nothing, the chances are it was harvested too early to ever ripen; if you smell something fermented or sour, it's likely the melon is already spoiling.

• Melons will continue to ripen slightly if left on the counter for a few days, but if left out longer, they may soften and ferment.

• Wash the outside of a melon with warm soapy water, then rinse before you cut into it—otherwise the knife's blade may drag bacteria into the flesh.

⤙ USE 'EM UP!

• Combine cantaloupes and honeydew with these foods and flavors: lime, chiles, almonds, mint, cilantro, balsamic vinegar, feta cheese, red onion, shrimp, crab, and cured ham.

• Sprinkle an underripe melon with a little lime juice, orange juice, or port to perk up its flavor.

• Overripe melons become mushy and watery, but if their flavor is still good (not sour or fermented), they're excellent for blending into smoothies or soups.

• Melons have such a high water content that it's difficult to cook with them. You can, however, give chunks a brief warming in a sauce (such as a light curry sauce) or take wedges for a quick trip over a very hot grill.

⤙ GOOD FOR YOU

These refreshing melons are packed with vitamin C and potassium.

CHERRIES

Vibrantly flavored, brilliantly colored, and almost as shiny as the summer sun itself, cherries are one of the most anticipated fruits of the year. The majority of the cherries that flood our markets each summer are Bing cherries—deep red, exceptionally juicy, and outstanding for both snacking and baking.

IN SEASON
June to August

⇥ CHOOSING & STORING

It pays to select your cherries one at a time; underripe, overripe, or damaged fruit will always disappoint, so choose carefully.
• Pick fruit that is very shiny, deep in color, and free of brown bruising or blemishes.
• Look for plump, bouncy cherries; very firm cherries may have been harvested too early, and soft ones (other than sour varieties) may be overripe.
• Choose the biggest fruits. Cherries gain most of their flavor and sugar content in the last days before harvesting, so larger usually means tastier.
• Select cherries still attached to the stem; they will remain fresher longer.
• Besides Bings, yellow varieties that sport just a spot of red blush, including Rainier and Queen Anne, are milder in flavor but excellent for snacking and baking. Small, soft sour cherries are sometimes available and are prized for baking and jam making but too tart for snacking.
• Refrigerate cherries in a plastic bag up to 3 days. You can also freeze them (pitted or unpitted) up to 6 months.

⇥ USE 'EM UP!

• Make the most of cherry season by investing in a pitter. You can also poke the pits out with a plastic drinking straw, but the straw will start to bend after a few dozen cherries.
• Choose yellow cherry varieties, and you'll save yourself from the dark, staining juices of deeper hued cherries. Yellow cherries are lovely in salads.
• Cherries pair beautifully with the flavors of almonds, tarragon, thyme, black pepper, fennel, apples, blueberries, brandy, chocolate, vanilla, and cheeses and other dairy products.
• Cherries—sour or sweet—make an exceptional sauce for pork, poultry, salmon, and game.
• A small amount of almond extract will brighten and heighten the flavor of cherries.

⇥ GOOD FOR YOU

Cherries rank high for their antioxidant content and are a valuable source of fiber, vitamin C, and potassium. Tart cherries might even help you get a good night's sleep as they contain melatonin, a hormone that may promote healthy sleep patterns.

CLEMENTINES

Small in size but big in flavor, these members of the mandarin orange family are one of the highlights of the citrus season. A ripe clementine's skin is thin and only loosely held to its flesh, making it a snap to peel and easy to separate into segments—one reason the fruit is wildly popular with children. Other mandarin varieties can also be used interchangeably with clementines, including larger, puffier tangerines and sweet satsumas.

⇥ CHOOSING & STORING
• Juiciness is a key aspect of the clementine's greatness, so look for signs that your fruit will please in this respect: It should be heavy in your hand, and the flesh should be smooth and glossy, not wrinkled or overly loose.
• Some clementines are sold with stem and a leaf or two attached. This can indicate freshness since long storage and ripening agents like ethylene usually cause the leaves to fall off.
• Look for small crates of clementines that appear in supermarkets around the holidays. Each 5-pound crate contains 2 to 3 dozen fruits, a great invitation to healthy snacking or a terrific host or hostess gift.
• Clementines will keep at room temperature 2 to 3 days or refrigerated for 1 to 2 weeks.

⇥ USE 'EM UP!
• Clementines are an absolute favorite for lunchboxes, road-trip noshing, teatime munching, and all-around blissful snacking. But they're an inspiration for cooking and baking too.
• The sweet-tart flavor of clementines is terrific paired with cinnamon, cardamom, ginger, soy sauce, shallots, chiles, mint, dill, cilantro, red onion, fennel, nuts, coconut, seafood, poultry, chocolate, and caramel.
• Start your morning with clementine sections as a natural sweetener for cereal, porridge, or yogurt.
• Add sectioned or chopped clementines to green salads and spinach salads, slaws, and grain dishes.
• Use chopped clementines or clementine juice in pan sauces or salsas for fish, shrimp, scallops, chicken, or pork.
• You can use clementines in just about any pastry or pudding that calls for oranges; substitute about 3 clementines for each orange called for.
• Want a superquick, sophisticated dessert for company? Place a bowl or platter of clementines on the table and serve small glasses of Port or dessert wine or cups of mint tea.

⇥ GOOD FOR YOU
Clementines are a delicious source of vitamin C, potassium, and fiber.

GRAPEFRUIT

Generous size, legendary juiciness, and a sunny sweet-tart flavor tempered by a hint of bitterness make grapefruit a favorite winter citrus. Better yet, they seem to have the ability to make just about any food they come in contact with taste fresher, so enjoy them in salads, salsas, and seafood and poultry dishes. Some tasty grapefruit relatives to look for include ugli fruit, pomelos, and tangelos.

IN SEASON
November to June

⇝ CHOOSING & STORING

- Look for skin that is smooth and supple with no signs of drying, wrinkling, or bruising.
- Avoid grapefruit that look like they have thick, puffy skin; these fruits are likely to have a lot of inedible pith, and are less flavorful and juicy than thin-skinned varieties.
- Russeting, or browning, on the skin will not affect flavor or quality.
- Store grapefruit at room temperature up to 1 week or loosely wrapped in the refrigerator for 2 to 3 weeks.
- Most grapefruit are classified as white, pink, or red (also called ruby), depending on the color of their flesh. White grapefruit is likely to be more tart and have more seeds than pink or red, but can be wonderfully juicy and flavorful, too.

⇝ USE 'EM UP!

Here's the challenge: Removing all the bitter pith and tough membranes to enjoy grapefruit's succulent sections. Try these strategies:

- **Classic breakfast grapefruit:** Halve a grapefruit. Free the fruit from the pith by cutting around the fruit with a sawing motion (a curved, serrated grapefruit knife is ideal for this). Now cut along the white membranes with a paring knife to release each section. Use a spoon to remove each section of flesh; a grapefruit spoon is perfect.
- **Easy peeling grapefruit:** Bring a saucepan of water to a boil. Drop in a grapefruit, remove the pan from the heat, cover, and let sit 5 minutes. Remove the fruit from the water, let it cool a few minutes, and then peel—all the pith should come away with the skin.
- **Grapefruit "supremes" for salads and salsas:** Cut a thin slice from the top and from the bottom of a fruit. Set it with one cut side flat on a cutting board and slice down along the curve of the fruit, removing all the peel and pith and cutting all the way to the flesh. Now hold the whole skinless fruit over a bowl and cut along the membranes to release each supreme, letting the segments and any juice drop into the bowl.

⇝ GOOD FOR YOU

A small red grapefruit packs about 76 mg of vitamin C—more than the recommended daily dose—plus the antioxidant lycopene.

GRAPES

Thousands of grape varieties are cultivated worldwide, the vast majority for making wine, vinegar, jelly, and raisins. Grapes sold for snacking are known as table grapes and are loosely classified as green, red, or black, and then again as seeded or seedless. Although seedless varieties are overwhelmingly popular, some purists insist that seeded varieties are superior in flavor: have fun tasting a few types of both and decide for yourself.

↳ CHOOSING & STORING

• Look for grapes in bunches with the fruit still firmly attached to the stem—a sign of freshness. Individual grapes should be plump with taut skin and no wrinkling; a powdery finish known as "bloom" on the skin of some varieties is an indication of freshness and careful handling.
• Grapes do not ripen further after picking; those harvested too early will be hard (not plump and juicy), small for their variety, and quite sour.
• Taste a grape before buying if you can—it's the best way to judge if the fruit is ripe and matches your preference for flavor and texture.
• Store grapes at room temperature 1 or 2 days; refrigerate them up to 1 week in a plastic bag or in the perforated plastic bag they came in.
• Grapes are one of the fruits with the most residual pesticides, so buy organic or rinse them thoroughly before eating.

↳ USE 'EM UP!

• Make grapes a dessert worthy of company by mounding bunches of different varieties on a platter. Choose contrasting colors, shapes, and sizes for dramatic appeal, and include a pair of small scissors or special grape shears so guests can help themselves to a few clusters.
• Freeze grapes for an icy treat: Cut small clusters from a bunch, rinse and pat dry, place on a sheet pan, and freeze until solid. Transfer to a zip-close plastic freezer bag and freeze up to 3 months.
• Grapes are fantastic in creamy salads like tuna salad, chicken salad, and salmon salad and an excellent addition to tossed salads; halve them to make spearing them with a fork easier.
• Grapes and mild cheeses are a favorite combination, but you can take this duo way beyond the cheese plate: Toss hot pasta with grapes and low-fat feta, blue cheese, or farmer's cheese; add halved grapes to your next grilled cheese sandwich; or try a goat cheese pizza topped with grapes, walnuts, and arugula.

↳ GOOD FOR YOU

You've probably heard of the health benefits associated with drinking red wine, and grapes contain many of the same antioxidants, including resveratrol.

KIWIFRUIT

Slice through a kiwifruit's unassuming brown skin and you'll be rewarded with enticing jewel-like green flesh dotted with black seeds. It's visually stunning, as well as delicious, contrasting creamy, sweet-tart flesh with a pleasant crunch from the fruit's small seeds. Keep an eye out for kiwi berries too: These grape-size fruits have smooth, edible skin, making them ideal for eating out of hand.

⇥ CHOOSING & STORING

Kiwifruit is harvested while still very firm, and slowly softens during ripening, increasing in sugar content and flavor.

• Choose hard or soft fruits with unblemished, fuzzy skin. Look at the stem end for wrinkling—a sign that the fruit is already too ripe.

• Cold retards ripening, allowing you to store firm kiwis in a plastic bag in the refrigerator for several weeks. Let them sit at room temperature for a few days and they'll become soft, juicy, and delicious.

• Speed ripening by placing kiwis in a paper bag with an apple.

⇥ USE 'EM UP!

• Try this easy way to peel a ripe kiwi: Cut a sliver off each end with a paring knife; then make a slit through the skin up the length of the fruit. Slip a metal soupspoon between the skin and the flesh, and work the spoon around the fruit, removing the skin in one neat piece.

• Kiwis are often relegated to garnishing fruit salads and bakery tarts, but they're outstanding as an eat-alone snack or the basis for tropical-tasting salsas, salads, sandwiches, and smoothies.

• Raw kiwifruit contains the protein-dissolving enzyme actinidin, the same enzyme found in pineapples. For this reason, never use uncooked kiwi as a marinade for meats, don't let it sit for any length of time with dairy, and don't try it with gelatin-based recipes.

• A sliced kiwi or two will add instant glamour to just about any dish: a salad, a pudding or tart, a sandwich, or even humble oatmeal. Try kiwis in smoothies or as a garnish for drinks, too.

⇥ GOOD FOR YOU

Kiwifruit is loaded with vitamin C and boasts a number of health-protective antioxidants.

LEMONS & LIMES

Just about nothing perks up a dish and brings our palate to attention like the brilliant, complex sourness of lemons and limes. Their culinary virtues are recognized around the world, so it's no wonder that the two varieties we find most commonly in our markets—Lisbon lemons and Persian limes—have many worthy relatives to experiment with, including sweet-tart Meyer lemons and diminutive Key limes.

IN SEASON
Year-round

➻ CHOOSING & STORING

• Select fruits with shiny, smooth skins of uniform color. Look for fruit with a plump appearance and a little give when pressed; rock-hard fruits are often dry and juiceless on the inside.

• If choosing from a number of fruits in a bin, opt for those that feel heaviest in your hand—they're likely to be juicier.

• You can leave lemons and limes at room temperature 3 to 4 days. They'll also keep loosely wrapped in the crisper drawer of your fridge for several weeks.

• Always wash these fruits well before using as the skins can harbor a number of contaminants. If you plan to use the zest, you may want to buy organic since pesticides are concentrated on the skins of conventionally grown fruit.

➻ USE 'EM UP!

• While lemons and limes can often be used interchangeably, the flavor of lime is typically associated with Mexican, Indian, and Southeast Asian cuisines, while lemon is more ubiquitous in European, Middle Eastern, North African, and North American dishes.

• Ever taste a soup, sauce, or other dish and find it just slightly flat? A squeeze of citrus juice might be the thing to brighten it up: Like salt, the acid in these fruits acts as a flavor enhancer.

• Lemon or lime juice is an easy way to boost the flavors of low-acid fruits like papaya, melon, avocado, and persimmons. The citric acid in the juice also helps stop the oxidation that causes the browning of cut apples, artichokes, avocados, and pears.

• To get more juice from your lemons and limes, roll them on the counter a few times to break up their juice sacks. Warmer fruit will also yield more juice, so microwave them 5 or 6 seconds.

• Don't forget the fruits' zest! Use it in dressings, sauces, batters, puddings, pasta dishes, grain salads, dips, preserves, or just about anywhere you want a bright citrus spark without the acid.

➻ GOOD FOR YOU

Turn to lemons and limes for a concentrated source of health-boosting vitamin C—people have been doing just that for centuries!

MANGOES

Mangoes are one of the world's favorite fruits, cultivated in just about every warm climate across the globe. Their popularity lags a bit here in the United States, but with rich, lusciously tropical flesh and a host of impressive health benefits, they're gaining fans fast. Mangoes are brilliant for snacking, but also ideal for incorporating into dishes both sweet and savory.

⇝ CHOOSING & STORING

- Skin color varies from variety to variety, so don't rely on it as a predictor of ripeness unless you're familiar with the type.
- Press mangoes gently at the stem end; a ripe mango should give slightly and smell sweet and tropical.
- Firm mangoes will ripen slowly at room temperature, although those harvested when immature and rock hard may never ripen properly.
- As they ripen, keep mangoes away from sunlight or very warm temperatures; both can adversely affect their flavor.
- Speed ripening by storing mangoes in a bag with an apple.
- Wrinkled skin, black splotches, and a fermented aroma are signs of overripe fruit.
- Freeze mangoes by peeling and dicing the flesh and placing it in zip-close plastic freezer bags or airtight containers.

⇝ USE 'EM UP!

- The bulk of a mango's flesh can be sliced away from the large, central pit in two "cheeks." You can slice the sides of the mango again to yield two smaller strips of flesh.
- Once you have removed the cheeks, score deep lengthwise and crosswise cuts into them, cutting almost to the skin; you should have a checkerboard of small squares. Push gently on the skin to turn the fruit slightly inside out, and then release the cubes of flesh with a paring knife or teaspoon. Alternatively, slice the cheeks into strips, and then use a paring knife to cut away the skin.
- Use diced mango in salads, chutneys, and salsas.
- Add sliced mango to sandwiches and wraps.
- Break out the blender and some plain fat-free yogurt and a few ice cubes, and you're a few pulses away from a delicious mango lassi.

⇝ GOOD FOR YOU

Mangoes are bursting with vitamins and minerals, including the antioxidants beta-carotene and lycopene. A cup of sliced mango provides vitamin A and almost all the vitamin C you'll need in a day. All that, and a respectable 3 grams of fiber as well.

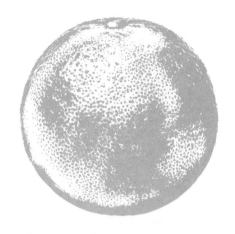

ORANGES

Nothing beats the cheery flavor and bright aroma of a really good orange. Better yet, they come into their peak during the cooler months when we can most appreciate both their sunny taste and immunity-boosting vitamin C. Navel oranges are the standard for peeling and eating, but also look for juicy Valencias, red-fleshed blood oranges, and complexly flavored Cara Cara oranges.

⇥ CHOOSING & STORING

One of life's small disappointments is peeling an orange in anticipation of a sweet, juicy treat and instead finding a dry, tasteless mass. Judging from the exterior alone can be difficult, but these tips and storage suggestions can help:

• Lift oranges before you buy them; heaviness for their size is usually a sign of juiciness.

• Don't rely on skin color alone; oranges are sometimes dyed to look more vibrant. Some greening on the skin will not affect quality, nor will rough brown patches known as russeting.

• Look for thicker skins on fruit that you want to peel, thinner skins on fruit you want to juice.

• Store oranges for several days at room temperature, but refrigerate them to keep them fresh for a week or more.

• Even if you're not planning to use the zest immediately, you can remove it before you peel an orange and freeze it. Use a zester or Microplane, wrap the zest securely in plastic wrap, and freeze it up to 3 months; add it to dressings, salads, baked goods, desserts, and drinks.

⇥ USE 'EM UP!

• To remove orange flesh in neat segments, first cut thin slices from both the top and bottom of a fruit. Set it on a cutting board and cut down along the curve of the fruit, removing all the peel and pith and cutting all the way to the flesh. Now hold the skinless fruit over a bowl and cut along the membranes to release each segment, letting the segments and any juice drop into the bowl.

• Want an easier method for preparing oranges for salads or desserts? Use a small serrated knife to remove the peel and white pith from the orange in a spiral. Halve the peeled orange lengthwise, then slice each half into thin half-moons, and remove any seeds.

• Oranges go exceptionally well with the flavors of spinach, lettuce, winter greens, fennel, onions, shallots, chiles, olives, seafood, poultry, chocolate, cinnamon, coconut, red wine, and almonds.

⇥ GOOD FOR YOU

In addition to an abundance of vitamin C, oranges pack heart-healthy potassium and magnesium and a variety of antioxidants.

PAPAYA

Even a single papaya plant can produce an abundant amount of fruit, making it a culinary staple in many tropical and semitropical parts of the world. When ripe, these pear-shaped fruits have rich, buttery flesh with a distinctively musky, floral flavor and low acid. The two main varieties you'll find are the very large (sometimes enormous!) fruits with orange flesh, and a smaller variety with rose-tinged flesh.

IN SEASON
year-round

↠ CHOOSING & STORING

• Tree-ripened papayas will have the deepest flavor, but this is one fruit that also ripens well off the tree. If your papaya is firm and green you can leave it at room temperature away from sunlight for several days and up to a week.
• A ripe papaya will have little or no green left on its skin, turning to yellow or orangey hues, and will give just slightly when pressed with your fingertip.
• Papayas have very delicate skins, so handle them gently. If the fruit was damaged in transport it may have brown cuts on the skins. As long as these are minimal, and no soft spots or mold are visible, this shouldn't affect the fruit's quality.
• Store ripe, cut fruit in the refrigerator for up to 2 days.

↠ USE 'EM UP!

• Split a papaya open and you'll find abundant round, black, slightly gelatinous seeds. Although edible, the seeds have a lightly bitter flavor and are usually discarded.
• Unripe, green papayas are a common ingredient in savory salads and pickles in many countries. The pale-green flesh is crisp and mildly flavored. Shred it to add to Southeast Asian slaws and salads.
• To enjoy a ripe, fragrant papaya at its simple best, split it, scrape out the seeds, and dig into the buttery soft flesh with a spoon. Add a squeeze of lemon or lime juice to heighten its flavor.
• A split papaya is also an excellent "boat" to hold a scoop of shrimp salad, tuna salad, or ham salad.
• Both green papaya and ripe papaya are an excellent base for salsa to serve with grilled pork, seafood, or tofu.

↠ GOOD FOR YOU

Papaya is a terrific source of vitamin C and also contains folate, fiber, and vitamin A.

PEACHES & NECTARINES

Summer's glorious peaches and nectarines are so similar in flavor and appearance that it's hardly surprising they're separated by a single gene (it's responsible for the fuzziness of peaches). Both fruits are commonly classified as either white or yellow, depending on the color of their flesh; some connoisseurs claim that the less common white fruit has a finer flavor.

IN SEASON
June to September

⇢ CHOOSING & STORING
• Opt for locally grown peaches and nectarines for best flavor and texture: They're more likely to have been ripened on the tree and less likely to have been bruised or mishandled in transport.
• Choose plump fruit with unblemished skin and no signs of bruising. Fruit harvested at proper ripeness will give slightly when pressed.
• Follow your nose! Flavorful peaches and nectarines should have a distinctly sweet, floral aroma; you should be able to detect their fragrance even when you're a few feet away.
• Leave peaches and nectarines at room temperature to soften, but be aware that they will not increase in sugar content or improve in flavor.
• Peaches and nectarines are two of the fruits with the most pesticide residue, so always rinse them well; better yet, buy organic when you can.

⇢ USE 'EM UP!
• Freestone peaches and nectarines are bred with a loose pit that is easily removable; simply cut through the fruit to the pit, turn the fruit to cut all the way around the pit, and then use your hands to twist the halves in opposite directions.
• Clingstone pits are more tenaciously fused to the fruits' flesh. You'll need to cut the flesh away from the pit.
• Fruit that's cooked will sometimes need to be peeled. To do so, score an X on the bottom of each, drop into boiling water for 15 seconds, and then transfer to a bowl of cold water to cool. The skin will rub off easily.
• Slice peaches and nectarines and add to savory salads, or dice them to use as the base for summery salsas.
• Cooking deepens and sweetens the flavor of peaches and nectarines, so turn on the stove or spark up the grill if you've got some fruit with less-than-outstanding flavor.
• Peaches and nectarines pair fabulously with herbs and spices, especially thyme, lavender, mint, ginger, cinnamon, and black pepper.

⇢ GOOD FOR YOU
Peaches and nectarines are a good source of potassium, fiber, niacin, and vitamin A.

PEARS

Bite into a truly ripe pear and it's hard not to smile as you reach for a few extra napkins. At their best, pears are sublimely sweet with rich, buttery flesh that fairly bursts with juice. And talk about versatile: They're just as delicious incorporated into savory dishes as sweet ones, and they cook up beautifully whether baked, broiled, poached, or grilled.

↠ CHOOSING & STORING

Commercially grown pears make a unique path to our tables. Harvested while still hard, they are "cured" in cold storage for several weeks and then brought to room temperature to complete ripening, a process that usually begins while the fruit is on your market's shelves and ends in your fruit bowl. Asian pears are an exception; this variety is generally fully ripened on the tree and should be eaten within a few days.

• Select pears that are free of soft spots, nicks, or cuts. Skin color varies from variety to variety, so don't use it as a gauge of ripeness unless you are familiar with the type.

• Unripe pears should be left at room temperature to ripen, a process that takes 2 to 6 days. Place them in a bag with an apple to speed ripening.

• Pears are ripe when they give just a little when pressed at the neck end and have a sweet, floral aroma when sniffed. Slightly underripe fruit will hold its shape better during cooking.

• Pears are one of the fruits with the most pesticide residue, so rub their skins well under running water before eating, or buy organic.

↠ USE 'EM UP!

• Enjoy pears at breakfast in cereal, over yogurt, or diced as a topping for pancakes or waffles.

• Make a quick pear compote by stewing diced pears (peeled or unpeeled) in a little bit of water or apple juice until soft. It's excellent with roast meats or as a dessert sauce.

• Poaching is a particularly good way to enjoy pears that are not quite ripe enough to eat raw. Wine or fruit juice are popular poaching liquids; classic flavorings include cloves, cinnamon sticks, star anise, orange peel, and rosemary.

• Asian pears should always be eaten raw as they have too high a water content to hold up to cooking; they're excellent in salads and on sandwiches.

• Pears are an outstanding complement to cheeses. Try them on a cheese plate, in salads, or as a dessert course topped with a soft cheese like goat cheese, ricotta, or mascarpone.

↠ GOOD FOR YOU

A medium pear packs an impressive 5 g of heart-healthy fiber.

anjou

Rounded and green, sometimes with a reddish blush; juicy, creamy, and very sweet

BEST FOR: Eating raw, slicing, baking

GOOD TO KNOW: Late-season pear with excellent flavor, sometimes known as the "Christmas pear"

asian

Round; yellow or russet skin; very crisp, mildly flavored, honey-sweet flesh with a lightly gritty texture

BEST FOR: Eating raw, slicing

GOOD TO KNOW: A high water content makes this pear a very refreshing snack

bartlett

Bell-shaped, with skin that turns from green to yellow when ripe; mild, juicy flesh with a smooth texture

BEST FOR: Eating raw, slicing

GOOD TO KNOW: Also known as Williams

forelle

Small, with deep yellow skin blushing to scarlet; very sweet, firm flesh

BEST FOR: Eating raw, slicing, baking, poaching, broiling

GOOD TO KNOW: Prized for their adorable size and bright color; firm flesh makes them good for cooking, although their small stature can make peeling and coring time-consuming

french butter

Bell-shaped, with golden russet skin; creamy, juicy flesh with sweet, spicy, caramel-like flavor

BEST FOR: Eating raw, slicing, broiling

GOOD TO KNOW: Less commonly available, but worth seeking out for its rich flavor and smooth texture

seckel

Small, with yellow-green flesh speckled with red; very crisp, sweet, and tangy

BEST FOR: Slicing, baking, broiling

GOOD TO KNOW: One of the smallest pear varieties, lovely for garnishing platters and cheese plates and popular in centerpieces

red bartlett

Bell-shaped, with skin that turns from brick to bright red when ripe; mild, juicy flesh with a smooth texture

BEST FOR: Eating raw, slicing

GOOD TO KNOW: A beautiful pear for salads and cheese plates; leave them unpeeled to enjoy their vivid color

bosc

Long, curved neck and russet gold skin; spicy, crunchy, and very firm

BEST FOR: Baking, poaching, broiling

GOOD TO KNOW: Good flavor and ability to keep its shape during cooking make it a top choice for poaching and broiling

comice

Large and rounded with yellow-green skin; honey-sweet, creamy flesh with intense floral flavor and aroma

BEST FOR: Eating raw, slicing

GOOD TO KNOW: One of the best choices for serving with cheese

red anjou

Rounded and deep red; juicy, creamy, and very sweet

BEST FOR: Eating raw, slicing, baking

GOOD TO KNOW: A beautiful pear for salads and cheese plates; leave them unpeeled to enjoy their vivid color

PINEAPPLE

Pineapple is so good raw that many cooks don't think about incorporating it into everyday cooking and baking, which is a shame: It's superb baked, broiled, grilled, stir-fried, and tossed into soups and salads. Just remember that fresh pineapple contains bromelain, an enzyme that breaks down protein, so don't add it to most dishes until just before serving and never use it with gelatin.

⇒ CHOOSING & STORING

• Contrary to popular belief, pineapples do not ripen after harvest, so spend a few moments to make sure the one you select is ready for eating.
• Give pineapples a sniff: They should have a rich, sweet, tropical aroma that will be strongest at the fruits' base.
• Look at the skin: It should be deeply colored and bright, although the hue (yellow, yellow-green, brown, or red) varies from variety to variety. It should give slightly when firmly pressed with your fingertip if the pineapple is ripe.
• Pineapple leaves should be crisp and green with no yellowing or browning at the tips. A center leaf should come out with a gentle tug if the fruit is ripe.
• Slightly underripe pineapples can be left at room temperature for a few days to soften, but remember that they will not increase in sugar content.
• Soft, ripe pineapples can be refrigerated for 3 to 4 days.

⇒ USE 'EM UP!

• To prepare a pineapple, first cut off the top and bottom. Set it on a cutting board and cut down to remove all the skin; use a paring knife to remove any small brown "eyes" set deeply into the flesh.
• For rings, cut the peeled pineapple into slices and remove the core of each with a small round cookie cutter.
• For chunks, slice the peeled pineapple lengthwise into quarters, then slice the core out of each quarter, and cut the flesh into the desired size.
• Many produce departments sell freshly peeled and cored pineapples, or you can try out any of a number of easy and effective peeling and coring gadgets.
• A medium pineapple will yield about 5 cups of diced flesh or 6 rings (each about ¾-inch thick).
• You don't have to discard the pineapple core. Even if you find it too fibrous to eat, try one of these yummy uses: Grate it and add it to slaws; cut it into long strips and use as swizzle sticks for seltzer; chop it and use it to infuse vodka; or stuff it into the cavity of a chicken before roasting.

⇒ GOOD FOR YOU

One cup of pineapple chunks provides a day's worth of vitamin C.

⇥CHOOSING & STORING

- Look for skins that are glossy and vividly colored; a blue-gray, powdery bloom is natural in most varieties and a sign of freshness.
- Ripe plums should be plump and feel tender and a little bouncy when pressed with your finger.
- Taste a plum, if possible, before buying a lot; it can be difficult to tell a juicy, flavorful plum from a mealy or bland one without getting under the skin.
- Store ripe plums in the refrigerator for a few days; underripe plums will soften if stored at room temperature for a day or two but will not become sweeter.

PLUMS

Large, juicy Japanese plums are the ones we usually eat out of hand in the summer months. They make thirst-quenching snacks and delicious desserts, and are excellent for just about anything raw—salads, salsas, and sandwich fillings. For baking and stewing, however, you'll want to choose the smaller, firmer, and tarter European plums; these excellent cooking fruits come in a variety of colors, from green and red to purple and blue-black.

⇥USE 'EM UP!

- The skins of plums are generally more sour than their flesh; although this is usually a pleasant contrast, peeling the fruit is advisable for some dishes, especially cooked ones.
- Peel plums neatly by scoring the bottom of each fruit with a small X, dropping it into boiling water for 15 seconds, and then transferring it to a bowl of cold water to cool. You should be able to remove the skin with your fingers or to gently scrape it off with the back of a paring knife.
- Strew sliced plums over cereal, yogurt, or ice cream. Sprinkle them with a little cinnamon or ground ginger to heighten their natural spicy flavor.
- Grill or sauté plums quickly and serve them with meats, poultry, or tofu; their flavor goes well with thyme, rosemary, shallots, and soy sauce.
- Also look for popular plum-apricot hybrids like pluots and plumcots; they can be exceptionally juicy and a revelation in honey-sweet flavor.

⇥GOOD FOR YOU

The skins of purple and black plums are an excellent source of the antioxidant chlorogenic acid.

POMEGRANATES

The tough, leathery exterior of a pomegranate hides hundreds of tiny jewel-like seeds, each bursting with bracing, sweet-tart juice. There are a few impediments to getting to these delectable treats, it's true, but anyone who perseveres will be richly rewarded. Or consider taking a shortcut—if your grocery offers them, buy a carton of already extracted seeds.

⤖ CHOOSING & STORING

- Hefting a few pomegranates will pay off: Fruit that feels heavy for its size is likely to be packed with juicy seeds.
- Look for pomegranates with vibrant, slightly glossy, plump skin with no sign of shrinking or wrinkling.
- Pomegranates are beautiful in a fruit bowl or as a centerpiece, but store them at room temperature for no more than a few days because they dry out quickly.
- Place pomegranates in a plastic bag and refrigerate for several weeks, depending on their condition.

⤖ USE 'EM UP!

Extracting the seeds from a pomegranate takes a little patience but is easy enough with these strategies:

- Cut off the crown of the pomegranate, slicing through the skin and white pith but not into the seed cavity.
- Score the exterior into quarters, again cutting deeply through the skin but not into the seeds.
- Drop the fruit into a large bowl of cold water and let it soak for 5 minutes. Holding the fruit below the surface of the water, break it into quarters along the lines you've scored, and then bend the skin and membrane gently away from the seeds.
- You can nibble the seeds away from the membrane, or if you want to separate them for use in recipes, work underwater again to carefully pry them out with your fingers. The seeds should sink and be easy to scoop up, while any white membrane should float to the top and can be discarded.
- Scatter pomegranate seeds over salads, drop into seltzer or other drinks, use as a garnish for pork and poultry dishes, or sprinkle over ice cream or other desserts.

⤖ GOOD FOR YOU

Pomegranate seeds are a good source of vitamin C, potassium, folate, and vitamin K.

RASPBERRIES

Raspberries make themselves at home with some of the world's most luxurious ingredients, including champagne and chocolate, but they often shine brightest when matched with humbler fare like yogurt, oatmeal, or a simple salad. Red berries are the norm, but golden and black raspberries are also available. Both variants can have a deeper, sweeter flavor than standard berries, but taste them before paying a premium to avoid disappointment.

►► CHOOSING & STORING

• Select deeply colored raspberries with no signs of bruising or mold.
• Check that raspberries are not still attached to the stem, a sign that they were harvested while still unripe and will be sour.
• Refrigerate berries for no more than 2 or 3 days to prevent molding; remove any damaged berries immediately, or they may affect the rest.
• Think ahead and freeze any berries you won't use before they go bad: Spread them on a baking sheet lined with parchment or wax paper and place in the freezer until solid, 1 to 2 hours. Store them in a zip-close plastic freezer bag up to 3 months.

►► USE 'EM UP!

• Add instant glamour to seltzer, ice tea, lemonade, or sparkling wine by dropping a few berries into your glass.
• Use raspberries as a garnish for salads, poultry, or pork dishes, or anything chocolate.
• Combine a few mashed raspberries and ½ cup champagne vinegar or rice wine vinegar in a glass jar; refrigerate for a few days, and you'll have delicious raspberry vinegar.
• Make a quick sauce for sweet or savory dishes: Puree berries in a food processor, adding a little water or orange juice if needed, and strain through a fine-mesh sieve.

►► GOOD FOR YOU

Raspberries are packed with fiber and vitamin C and contain a number of antioxidants, including ellagic acid.

STRAWBERRIES

Heralding an end to the dark days of winter and the arrival of spring, the emergence at markets of juicy, aromatic, ruby-red strawberries is a welcome sign of good things to come. During berry season, be sure to look out for wild strawberries at farmers' markets—these small wonders make up for what they lack in stature in sweetness and flavor.

IN SEASON
April to July

➡ CHOOSING & STORING
• Look for strawberries that are firm, free of mold, and deep red with fresh green caps.
• Avoid berries that have green or white patches around the stem—a sign they are not fully ripe. Once picked, berries do not continue to ripen.
• If purchasing berries in packages, check that they are not so tightly packed that they have bruised. Likewise, check the bottom of the container for any excess moisture or staining.
• To store, remove berries from the container and discard any that are damaged. Return the unwashed, unhulled berries to the container, or spread them out on a paper towel–lined plate and loosely cover with plastic wrap. Refrigerate berries up to 2 days.
• Gently rinse and hull berries just before serving. If serving whole, you may want to leave the caps intact—the green-red contrast looks great!
• Strawberries freeze well. Gently rinse, pat dry, and arrange them on a tray in a single layer. Freeze and transfer to a zip-close plastic freezer bag. Frozen berries will keep 3 to 6 months.

➡ USE 'EM UP!
• To revitalize the flavor of "tired" berries, sprinkle with 1 teaspoon each sugar and fresh lemon juice per cup and let sit for 20 minutes.
• The classic accompaniment to bowls of fresh strawberries is cream, but Greek yogurt is wonderfully satisfying with them as well!
• Not only are strawberries a star in fruit salads, but you can also add them to leafy green salads as well, or toss with a light balsamic dressing and a few chopped veggies for a savory side dish.
• Use strawberries as a garnish for cereals, pancakes, waffles, cakes, frozen desserts, or sparkling drinks—they'll add flavor and eye appeal.
• Strawberries are ideal in sorbets, frozen yogurts, parfaits, smoothies, cold soups, tarts, and dessert sauces and as a filling for strawberry shortcake.

➡ GOOD FOR YOU
One cup of berries contains 90 mg of vitamin C, more than the recommended daily intake for an adult. They're also packed with potassium, contain a good amount of fiber, and offer a number of potent antioxidants.

WATERMELON

It's no surprise that the watermelon—considered by many to be the quintessential sweet, cooling antidote to the dog days of summer—originated in Africa, where it was prized not only for its flavor but also its ability to serve as a source of hydration. In the New World, Native Americans and settlers fully embraced this versatile melon, cultivating over 50 varieties.

➼ CHOOSING & STORING

• Watermelons range in size from small round ones like Sugar Baby to giant elongated ones such as Charleston Gray. Yellow-fleshed watermelons are also sometimes available, several varieties of which are bred for extra sweetness.

• Seedless melons have become overwhelmingly popular, but seeds are so easy to remove that you should let flavor and ripeness be your guide when selecting a melon.

• Look for smooth, unblemished skin with deep color. One side of the melon may be paler than the rest, indicating that part of the rind was resting on the ground while ripening on the vine.

• Fragrance is important; a ripe melon should smell fresh and sweet. When tapped, it should sound taut and hollow if ripe.

• If you purchase a piece of a cut watermelon, look for firm flesh with deep color and dark seeds.

• Before storing or cutting watermelon, rinse the exterior well under cold running water. This will keep your knife from dragging any bacteria that may be on the skin into the flesh of the melon.

• You can store whole watermelon at room temperature 7 to 10 days or in the refrigerator for 2 to 3 weeks. Cut melon will keep covered and refrigerated for 2 to 3 days.

➼ USE 'EM UP!

• Watermelon is 92 percent water, so it's no wonder it's ideal as a base for frozen desserts like ices, sorbets, and granitas.

• Pureed watermelon combines well with other fruit juices and yogurt to make tasty smoothies and with seltzer and lime for a thirst quencher. It also lends itself to summer soups and salsas.

• Savory watermelon salads have become a summer classic. Some complementary ingredients to consider in a salad include red onion, cucumber, tomato, jicama, scallions, mint, basil, feta, goat cheese, Kalamata olives, green pumpkin seeds, lime, and champagne vinegar.

➼ GOOD FOR YOU

Watermelon is a good source of vitamins A and C, and is packed with the antioxidant lycopene.

VEGGIES

ARTICHOKES

These relatives of the roadside thistle are an Italian staple that's become an American mainstay. The large greenish-purple globe artichokes are most common. You may also see smaller ones known as baby artichokes, although they are not actually babies: An artichoke's size is determined by its location on the plant's stalk; those at the top will be the largest, while those at the base will be smaller.

⇥ CHOOSING & STORING
• Look for firm artichokes with tightly furled leaves and plump, not dried out, stems.
• If squeezed, a fresh artichoke should offer good resistance, and the leaves should "squeak" slightly as they rub against each other.
• Brown spots or a rusty tinge on the outer leaves of an artichoke means that it has been exposed to cold, something that shouldn't affect its flavor or texture. In fact, some connoisseurs claim that these "frosted" or "winter-kissed" artichokes are particularly tasty and tender (you be the judge!).
• Store artichokes in the coolest part of the refrigerator wrapped loosely in paper or plastic.

⇥ USE 'EM UP!
Cleaning a fresh artichoke for cooking is not a daunting task. No special skill is required, just a little time, a small sharp knife, and a bowl of cold water to which you've added the juice of half a lemon. Once cleaned, you'll drop the artichokes into this acidulated water to prevent browning.
• To prepare an artichoke for cooking whole: Peel off the dark, tough petals around the base of the artichoke until you get to the petals that are lighter in color. Cut off the very top of the artichoke, cutting just below the prickly tips of the petals. Use a pair of kitchen scissors to snip off any prickly tips lower on the artichoke. Peel the tough skin off the stem with your paring knife and trim the bottom. If you need the artichokes to sit level, you may cut off the stem entirely, but don't discard it—cook it along with the artichokes.
• To prepare an artichoke heart: Run a paring knife around the base of the artichoke, removing all petals until you get to the tender petals with yellow-green bottoms. Slice off all but 1 inch of the top of the artichoke. Use a teaspoon or melon baller to scoop out the small petals and hairy choke at the center of the artichoke, exposing the heart. Peel the stem and leave it on, or separate it from the base of the heart.

⇥ GOOD FOR YOU
Artichokes have been prized since ancient times for a host of medicinal powers, and modern science gives us reasons to love them, too. They're a good source of potassium, folate, and fiber, and contain a number of antioxidants.

ARUGULA

It may look like a lettuce, but arugula is actually a member of the cruciferous vegetable family, a nutritionally powerful group that includes broccoli, cabbage, and kale. Its peppery flavor makes a bold statement in salad mixes or on its own. It's less commonly (but just as deliciously!) wilted into pastas, soups, and other hot dishes, or steamed or sautéed like spinach.

⇥ CHOOSING & STORING

• Look for crisp, dark green leaves without yellowing, a sign of age, or slimy spots, indicating poor handling.

• In general, small "baby" leaves will be tender and mild in flavor, while larger leaves will be crisper and have a pronounced peppery bite. Choose according to your preference.

• Handle arugula gently from market to kitchen to refrigerator in order to avoid bruising its fragile leaves. Arugula packaged in plastic "clamshells" has the benefit of being protected from crushing.

• Larger leaves are often sold in a bunch held together with a twist tie or rubber band. Remove the tie or band, then separate the leaves, and discard any that look yellowed or wilted. Wrap the root ends in a damp paper towel, and then store the whole bunch in a plastic bag.

• Use arugula within 1 or 2 days to enjoy its distinctively fresh, pungent flavor at its best.

• Arugula is grown in sandy soil, so it's important to rinse it very well before using, even if it comes in a package labeled "prewashed."

⇥ USE 'EM UP!

• Arugula is best known as a salad green, and with good reason: Its crisp texture and mild but assertive bite is terrific on its own, or it can be mixed with any number of other greens. It's also a natural for grain or pasta salads.

• Dress it with a light vinaigrette, and arugula makes a tasty and attractive bed for fish, shellfish, sliced meat or poultry, or braised vegetables.

• Toss arugula into hot pasta until it wilts for a bright, lightly spicy addition.

• Take advantage of arugula's herbal side by using it in pesto or sprinkling it on top of grilled or sautéed cutlets or chops.

• Arugula is excellent in sandwiches (try it in a grilled cheese!) and wraps, and is a favorite for topping pizza.

⇥ GOOD FOR YOU

A cup of arugula has just 5 calories and contains vitamins A and K and folate.

ASPARAGUS

Green, white, and purple—whatever variety you prefer, the color of asparagus is more about pleasing your plate than your palate. Fact is, all varieties and sizes—pencil (very thin), medium, or jumbo—taste pretty much the same. Focus on finding the freshest stalks and you won't be disappointed: Locally harvested asparagus is a revelation in spring flavor.

↦ CHOOSING & STORING

• Look for asparagus with straight, firm stalks. The tips should be tightly closed and free of slime. The cut ends should appear fresh, not woody or wrinkled. Give asparagus the sniff test: It should smell fresh and earthy, not sour.
• Pick the size to match your cooking technique. Skinny pencil stalks cook very quickly and are ideal for pasta, risotto, and other dishes where you don't want them to overwhelm the flavors of other ingredients. Choose medium or jumbo stalks for steaming, roasting, and grilling.
• Most bunches of asparagus weigh between 1 and 2 pounds. If you need a specific weight for a recipe, weigh it in the market.
• Think fresh: Asparagus begins losing its sweetness from the moment it's harvested. Keep it refrigerated no more than 2 to 3 days. Wrap it loosely in plastic or paper, or place the cut ends in a jar with 1 or 2 inches of water in the bottom (like a bunch of flowers) and cover the exposed stalks loosely with plastic wrap.

↦ USE 'EM UP!

• White asparagus is popular in Europe, where it is prized for its sweetness and tenderness. But beware: The white variety turns bitter with age so buy it and cook it the same day.
• Think twice before plunking down a fortune for purple asparagus: It's almost identical to green asparagus in flavor, and turns green during cooking, losing all but a tinge of its distinctive violet hue. If it's very fresh, try it in a raw preparation to enjoy its color.
• Bend the stalks near the base of pencil or medium asparagus, and the woody part of the stalk will snap off.
• Don't use this snap technique for jumbo stalks; you'll lose up to half of the vegetable you paid for. Instead, cut off just the white base of the stalk, then use a vegetable peeler to remove the first couple of inches of tough skin on the stalk.
• If you find very fresh, crisp stalks, be sure to try asparagus raw: Shave it thinly with a vegetable peeler and toss it in a light lemony dressing.

↦ GOOD FOR YOU

Asparagus is an excellent source of vitamin K and contains impressive amounts of folate.

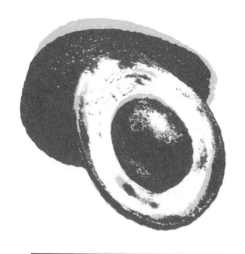

AVOCADOS

Rich and buttery with a hint of sweetness and almost no acid, the avocado has such a unique flavor profile for a fruit that it's usually treated as a vegetable. The most common variety in the United States is the Hass, easily recognizable by its very dark green, almost black skin with a rough, pebbly texture. Jade-green, smoother-skinned Fuerte and Florida avocados are milder in flavor, with flesh that is less buttery.

IN SEASON
year-round

⇥ CHOOSING & STORING
• Look for avocados with unblemished skins that feel heavy for their size.
• Press the fruit gently near the stem end with your finger tip: If it's rock-hard, it may take up to a week to ripen; if it offers just a little give, it will ripen within about 3 days; and if your finger leaves a slight indentation, it's already ripe.
• Use avocados only when they're ripe; unripe avocados are nearly tasteless.
• Store unripe avocados at room temperature and ripe ones in the refrigerator for 1 or 2 days.
• Speed the ripening of avocados by placing them in a paper bag with an apple; leave at room temperature and they should be soft in 1 to 3 days.
• Keep avocados from browning by brushing the cut surfaces with lemon or lime juice; although unattractive, browning will not affect the flavor or texture.

⇥ USE 'EM UP!
• To halve and pit an avocado, run a knife lengthwise all the way around, cutting right to the pit in the middle. Twist the halves in opposite directions, separating them. Remove the pit either by prodding and loosening it with a spoon and then scooping it out, or by giving the pit a firm whack with the blade of a heavy knife and lifting the pit out.
• Use avocados' natural richness to enhance smoothies, sandwiches, salsas, salads, dressings, omelets, cold soups, ceviche, and tacos.
• Diced avocado makes a great garnish for chili, hot soup, baked or grilled fish, chicken cutlets, and fruit salad.

⇥ GOOD FOR YOU
A powerful combination of monounsaturated fats, potassium, and vitamin E makes avocados an excellent food choice for promoting heart and skin health. They are, however, one of the very few fruits that have a SmartPoints value: One thick slice (about ⅛ of a medium Hass avocado) or 1½ tablespoons mashed have a SmartPoints value of 1, so enjoy their rich flavor and great nutritional benefits in moderation.

BEETS

Once considered staid, stodgy, or just downright unappetizing, beets have undergone a culinary renaissance. Vibrant, earthy-tasting red beets are the most commonly available, but specialty stores and farmers' markets now offer a dazzling array of colors and sizes that are worth seeking out during the summer and fall season.

⇥ CHOOSING & STORING
- Look for beets that are firm, not flabby, with skin that is free of cuts and discoloration.
- Small or medium beets are usually sweeter and more tender than larger beets, so try to buy beets no larger than baseballs.
- Sweet, mild golden beets won't stain your hands or cutting board as aggressively as red beets, making them a good choice for using raw in salads and slaws. Also look for whimsical white-and-red-striped candy cane, or Chioggia, beets, which are almost always sold while still small.
- If the beet greens are attached, they should be bright green and fresh looking. The greens will leach moisture from your beets, so cut them off about a ½ inch above the beet top before storing.
- Place beets in a plastic bag and refrigerate up to several weeks. Greens should be wrapped in a paper towel, placed in a paper bag, and refrigerated no more than 1 or 2 days.

⇥ USE 'EM UP!
- Trim and peel beets after cooking, not before, so their juices (and some nutrients) won't bleed out.
- Roasting concentrates beets' flavor and sweetness, and is super simple. Just wrap the beets in foil, and place on the rack of a 375°F oven until tender, 30 to 60 minutes depending on size. Let cool and rub skins off with a paper towel.
- Raw beets are a fabulous addition to salads and slaws. One of the best ways to prepare raw beets is to shred them on the large holes of a box grater or with a food processor.
- Removing red beet juice stains from cutting boards is difficult; speed cleanup by covering your board with parchment paper before chopping beets. You can keep your hands from getting stained by wearing disposable latex gloves.

⇥ GOOD FOR YOU
In addition to healthy amounts of folate, magnesium, potassium, and fiber, beets are a unique source of antioxidants called betalains. And don't forget to use beet greens—they're a good source of vitamins A and K.

BELL PEPPERS

Bell peppers come in a rainbow of colors, including the common red, yellow, and green varieties as well as orange, brown, purple, and more. Depending on how they are grown, bell peppers are referred to as either Holland peppers, raised in greenhouses, or field peppers, grown outdoors. Also look for bags of sweet, colorful mini peppers.

IN SEASON

Holland peppers year-round; field peppers June to October

➤ CHOOSING & STORING

• Look for peppers with smooth, shiny skin and a stem end that looks fresh and green, not brown or dried out.
• Holland peppers have a higher water content than field peppers and will be quite heavy and often startlingly expensive. The good news is that they are available year-round and are uniformly excellent in flavor and texture.
• Store bell peppers in a plastic bag in the refrigerator for up to 1 week. Or seed and dice peppers and freeze them up to 3 months.
• New to the market are sweet mini peppers, a remarkable thumb-size hybrid in red, yellow, and orange; in addition to cuteness, few seeds and a high sugar content have made them popular.

➤ USE 'EM UP!

• Roasting intensifies peppers' sweetness and makes them an ideal base for soups and sauces. To roast peppers whole, place them on a parchment-lined baking sheet and cook in a 425°F oven until skins are browned and blistered, 15 to 20 minutes. Transfer peppers to a paper bag, seal the bag, and cool 10 to 20 minutes. Remove the stem and seeds, and rub the skin off the peppers; you can do this easily under running water, although you'll lose some of the flavor.
• You can also grill peppers over a medium-hot grill for about 10 minutes, turning frequently; cool and clean them in the same way as roasted peppers (see above).

➤ GOOD FOR YOU

All bell peppers are packed with vitamins and minerals, and certain colors have even more of the good stuff than others. A yellow pepper has more than twice the amount of vitamin C as a green bell pepper; orange and red peppers contain more of the antioxidant beta-carotene than the green variety; and red peppers contain the powerful antioxidant lycopene.

BROCCOLI

Delicious, versatile, and outrageously healthful—there's a lot to love about broccoli. Visit a farmers' market in the fall for broccoli at its crispest and sweetest—a real treat! Broccoli also has a few relatives you should look out for. Broccolini is a hybrid variety with slender stems topped with a single flower cluster. And the Italian favorite broccoli rabe is another delicious, versatile family member.

IN SEASON
October to February

⇥ CHOOSING & STORING

- Look for broccoli with firm, dark green to purple-green floret clusters without yellow blossoms, a sign of age.
- Give it the sniff test: Broccoli should smell fresh and earthy, not sour or cabbage-like.
- Refrigerate broccoli in a paper or plastic bag in the vegetable drawer of your refrigerator. Although broccoli will keep a fresh appearance for a week or more, it rapidly becomes bitter and woody, so try to use it within a few days for best flavor.

⇥ USE 'EM UP!

- Overcooking can turn the freshest broccoli into a khaki-colored, tasteless mush. Keep cooking times short to preserve its flavor and famously crisp texture.
- Cut florets into uniform size and cook only until they turn bright green and stems are barely flexible. That means just 4 to 5 minutes of steaming or grilling, about 3 minutes of sautéing, and about 2 minutes of boiling or microwaving.
- Don't overlook eating broccoli raw; it's a crunchy classic on crudité platters and wonderfully refreshing as the base for a vegetable salad.
- Remember that even broccoli's thick, sometimes woody, stalks are edible—and delicious. Separate the stalk from the crown, trim the base, and peel off the thick, fibrous skin and you'll have a tender bit of juicy flesh. You can slice it and cook it along with the florets, munch it raw, or grate it for salads, slaws, or soups.

⇥ GOOD FOR YOU

One cup of steamed broccoli contains as much fiber as a slice of whole wheat bread. In addition, broccoli is packed with vitamin C, and contains a terrific amount of heart-healthy potassium, plus iron and vitamins A and B_6.

BRUSSELS SPROUTS

There was a time that Brussels sprouts got pretty short shrift: They'd make an annual appearance on the Thanksgiving table, and then go underground again for another year. Thankfully things have changed, and these diminutive cabbages now appear year-round on restaurant menus and in home-cooked meals alike.

IN SEASON
November to January

►► CHOOSING & STORING
• Look for firm, uniformly sized Brussels sprouts with no (or minimal) browning of the base or yellowing of the outer leaves.
• Smaller sprouts will generally be sweeter and more tender.
• Take a pass on pale green sprouts; the color may be a sign that the darker outer leaves have been stripped off to hide the signs of age or improper handling.
• Buy sprouts that are sold still clustered along their large heavy stalk if you see them available. Not only does the stalk make a fabulous conversation piece but the sprouts will keep longer and are likely to taste phenomenally fresh when you cook them.
• Store sprouts wrapped first in a paper towel and then loosely in plastic

►► USE 'EM UP!
• Rinse Brussels sprouts and remove any discolored outer leaves. Cut a thin sliver off the base of the sprouts' stems if they are browned.
• Scoring the bottom of each stem with an X will help heat penetrate the core of the sprout, making for more even cooking.
• Large sprouts (those as big as Ping-Pong balls) should be halved before cooking; smaller ones can be left whole.
• Cook sprouts just until crisp-tender, no longer. A fork should meet just a little resistance when poked into the stem end of a properly cooked sprout.
• Brussels sprouts are wonderful raw. Thinly slice them and use them as a base for salads or slaws or as a garnish for sandwiches or tacos.

►► GOOD FOR YOU
Brussels sprouts are a good source of folate, vitamins C and K, and fiber.

CABBAGE

Think you know cabbage? Most of us are familiar with the head cabbages (green, white, red, and Savoy) because they serve as the base for staple dishes like coleslaw, sauerkraut, and stuffed cabbage. Less familiar are loose-leaf cabbages like bok choy, Napa, and a myriad of sturdy to feathery cabbages popular in Asian cuisines. These members of the Brassica group have diverse and delicious culinary uses, but all share similar nutritional qualities.

IN SEASON
Year-round

⇥ CHOOSING & STORING

• Look for very dense heads of cabbage with glossy, crisp, tightly packed leaves. There should be no sign of browning at the base of the head or on the leaves.
• Loose-leaf cabbages like bok choy and choy sum should have crisp, unblemished stems and soft, fresh-looking leaves.
• Cabbage is famous for keeping well; uncut head cabbage can be refrigerated, loosely wrapped in plastic, for weeks; loose-leaf varieties like bok choy and choy sum will keep 3 or 4 days.

⇥ USE 'EM UP!

• Remove any curled, browned, or wilted leaves from cabbage. Rinse the outer leaves of head cabbages and all the leaves of loose-leaf cabbages; blot dry.
• For head cabbage, cut the entire head lengthwise into halves or quarters; then cut out and discard the thick white inner core.
• Shred cabbage for slaws or salads on the large holes of a box grater or with the slicing blade of a food processor, or simply thinly slice with a sharp knife, preferable for loose-leaf cabbages.
• To remove leaves whole for stuffing, do not cut the cabbage; submerge the entire head in a very large pot of boiling water and cook until the outer leaves are flexible, 2 to 3 minutes. Immediately drain and cool the cabbage under cold running water. The outer leaves should peel off easily.
• Cabbage is famous for pickling well, and is the main ingredient for some of the world's favorite fermented dishes like sauerkraut and kimchi. You can make a quick homemade cabbage pickle by covering sliced cabbage with a hot brine of vinegar, water, sugar, and salt; after it cools, refrigerate it up to 2 weeks and use as a garnish for sandwiches, tacos, soups, and more.

⇥ GOOD FOR YOU

Cabbage is rich in vitamin K and a source of vitamin C and fiber. Each variety has a slightly different nutrient profile, so incorporate as many types into your diet as possible for optimum health benefits.

baby bok choy

Small, loose heads with squat, pale green leaves and crunchy stems; sweet and mildly mustard-like flavor

BEST FOR:
Salads, grilling, steaming, braising

GOOD TO KNOW:
Very small heads are best cooked whole; heads over 6 inches long can be split before cooking

bok choy

Tall heads with thick, juicy, ivory-colored stalks and tender, green leaves; sweet, mildly earthy flavor

BEST FOR:
Salads, grilling, stir-frying, soups

GOOD TO KNOW:
Leaves will cook faster than stems, so consider separating the two and adding stems first, leaves toward the end of cooking

napa

Glossy, loose heads of long, slightly crinkled leaves; mild to strong cabbage flavor

BEST FOR:
Salads, slaws, stir-fries, soups, kimchi

GOOD TO KNOW:
Also known as Chinese cabbage

red

Dense, crisp, brilliant-purple or magenta heads; mild to strong cabbage flavor

BEST FOR:
Salads, slaws, braising, stir-frying

GOOD TO KNOW:
Cooking this cabbage with acidic ingredients like wine, vinegar, or lemon juice will help preserve its vibrant color

choy sum

Thick stems with tender, dark green leaves and small yellow flowers; earthy flavor

BEST FOR:
Steaming, stir-frying, soups

GOOD TO KNOW:
Prepare for cooking as you would broccoli rabe

savoy

Looser heads of crinkly, deep green leaves; mild flavor

BEST FOR: Salads, braising, stir-frying, stuffed leaves

GOOD TO KNOW:
The attractive texture of the leaves makes them a favorite for stuffing

green

Dense, crisp, apple green heads; mild to strong cabbage flavor

BEST FOR:
Salads, slaws, braising, stir-frying, stuffed leaves

GOOD TO KNOW:
Excellent cut into thick wedges and braised

white

Dense, crisp, very pale green heads; very mild cabbage flavor

BEST FOR: Slaws, sauerkraut

GOOD TO KNOW:
The classic cabbage for sauerkraut and pickling

tatsoi

Small, very loose heads of round, crisp, forest green leaves

BEST FOR: Salads, soups, braising

GOOD TO KNOW:
A common addition to mesclun salad mixes

CARROTS

Carrots are as delicious raw as they are cooked, and so versatile that they're found in almost every cuisine worldwide. They often play a supporting role in stocks, stews, and salads, but they're also delightful as the main event. Better still, their naturally sweet flavor and vibrant color make them just as popular with children as with adults. Visit farmers' markets to find carrots at their fresh, flavorful, aromatic best.

↦ CHOOSING & STORING

- Look for smooth, moist skins on carrots, a sign of freshness.
- Avoid overly large "horse carrots"; they're usually woody and tasteless.
- If carrots are sold with tops attached, they should be sprightly and green with no sign of yellowing or wilting. Remove the tops before storing as they will drain the carrots of moisture.
- Buy bagged, peeled baby-cut carrots carefully; sniff the bag first to make sure it smells fresh, not sour; then pinch a carrot through the bag to see that it feels firm and dry, not slimy.
- Consider buying organic because carrots are among the vegetables with the highest pesticide residues. Pesticides are concentrated in the skin, so peeling conventionally grown carrots is recommended even though it will decrease the vegetable's nutrient levels somewhat.
- Store carrots in a plastic bag in the refrigerator up to 1 week.

↦ USE 'EM UP!

Carrots are a dream in the kitchen: They're excellent raw, almost impossible to overcook, and work with just about every flavor palate we know. Try these sweet and savory tricks:

- Grate raw carrots to add to slaws, salads, soups, pilaf, and even meat loaf or pasta sauce. Mix grated carrots with dried fruits and nuts, and serve over yogurt or oatmeal.
- Grated raw carrots also enhance muffin, pancake, and quick-bread batters. They'll even fit into many cookie and candy recipes.
- Slice carrots into thin coins for use in stir-fries, soups, stews, and casseroles.
- Lay large carrots across the bottom of a roasting pan to make a flavorful, edible "rack" for a whole fish or a lean pork or beef roast.
- If you have very fresh carrot tops, use them like dill to garnish salads, soups, or cooked carrots.
- A 1-pound bunch or bag of carrots will contain 5 to 6 medium carrots. A medium carrot will yield approximately ⅔ cup sliced or grated carrot.

↦ GOOD FOR YOU

Carrots are packed with vitamin A and B vitamins and are a good source of fiber.

CAULIFLOWER

There's a lot to love about cauliflower: Nutty and sweet, it has a crunchy, pleasantly crumbly texture when raw, but with cooking turns so velvety smooth that it's often used as a stand-in for mashed potatoes. Pure white or ivory heads are the norm, although pale green, purple, and orange varieties, almost identical in flavor to white, are sometimes available, as are diminutive heads known as baby cauliflower.

▸▸ CHOOSING & STORING

- Avoid cauliflower with brown or gray spotting, a sign of age or water damage.
- Look for heads that are very dense with tightly clustered "curds."
- Green leaves at the base of the head should be crisp and fresh-looking.
- Refrigerate cauliflower loosely wrapped in a paper or a plastic bag no more than 2 to 3 days.
- Always store cauliflower stem side down to keep condensation from forming on the head and affecting its color or texture.
- A close cousin to cauliflower is the striking Romanesco, a lime-green head with fantastically whorled, magical-looking florets. Despite its exotic looks, Romanesco tastes and cooks up almost identically to white cauliflower.

▸▸ USE 'EM UP!

- Avoid a cabbage-like flavor and aroma by keeping cauliflower's cooking time short.
- Add some drama to dinner by steaming or roasting a head of cauliflower whole; cook until the core is just tender when pierced, place on a platter, and cut into wedges at the table.
- Roast cauliflower until it is lightly browned to make the most of its sweetness and nuttiness.
- Steam and puree cauliflower for a delectable alternative to mashed potatoes.
- Many people enjoy crunchy cauliflower florets raw in salads or on a crudité plate, although others find it too musty when uncooked. If you belong to the latter group, blanch the florets in boiling water for 60 seconds, cool under cold water, pat dry, and enjoy.
- Cauliflower is wonderful plain, but it also has a great affinity for very strong flavors like cumin, curry, ginger, garlic, chiles, olives, capers, and blue cheese.

▸▸ GOOD FOR YOU

Glucosinolates, the sulfur-containing compounds in cauliflower, may protect the body against a number of diseases, including some cancers.

CELERY

If you think there's anything plain, lowly, or too "diet-like" about celery, you need to revisit this complex, versatile veggie. Not only does it deliver one of the best crunches in the vegetable kingdom, it also packs an outstandingly fresh, herbal flavor that's as good raw as it is cooked. And don't forget the value of celery's feathery, light green leaves: use them as you would parsley for bright, herblike flavor.

IN SEASON
year-round

⤷ CHOOSING & STORING

- Try to buy celery with leaves attached; soft, unwilted leaves are a sign of freshness. If the tops have been lopped off, the ends should look freshly cut, not brown or dried out.
- Look for plump outer stalks that are very light green to yellow; avoid bunches with dark green and fibrous-looking stalks, which are likely to be bitter.
- Gently bend a stalk; fresh celery should be crisp and rigid, not rubbery, and should snap rather than flex.
- Store celery in the vegetable drawer of your fridge loosely wrapped in plastic for a week or more. Keep it away from the coldest part of the refrigerator; its high water content makes it likely to freeze.
- Buy organic celery when possible because it is one of the vegetables with the highest pesticide residue.

⤷ USE 'EM UP!

- Rinse celery stalks very well before using; rinsing will remove any dirt or grit trapped at the base of the stalks and will also help remove pesticides from nonorganic celery.
- Outer stalks are the most fibrous and have the most pronounced anise-like flavor, making them ideal for stocks, soups, and other long-cooked dishes. They may be peeled with a vegetable peeler to remove the toughest fibers.
- The tender inner stalks, known as the heart, are better for eating raw in salads, slaws, or crudités; they have a mild, extremely fresh flavor and excellent crispness.
- Don't overlook cooking a bunch of celery whole; it's a flavorful, meltingly tender side dish when braised in a little chicken or vegetable stock or roasted with a drizzle of olive oil or sesame oil and a sprinkle of sea salt.

⤷ GOOD FOR YOU

Celery is a good source of vitamin K, which may help to promote bone health.

CELERY ROOT

The look of a whole celery root—knobby, dusty, or downright dirty, and fringed with hair-like roots—can be less than appealing to the cook. But take heart: All you need is a heavy knife and a little patience to transform it into one of the most versatile and intriguing members of the root vegetable family. You might also find this vegetable marketed under two of its other monikers, celeriac or knob celery.

IN SEASON
October to February

⇥ CHOOSING & STORING

• Select medium-size knobs when possible. Very large heads (those larger than a softball) may be tough, while small ones (about the size of a tennis ball) may not yield much flesh after peeling.
• Older celery roots may develop a spongy or hollow center and lose flavor, so choose roots that feel dense and have no soft spots.
• Store celery root in a loosely closed paper or plastic bag in the vegetable drawer of your refrigerator 1 to 2 weeks.

⇥ USE 'EM UP!

• Choose a sturdy, sharp knife to trim a knob of celery root. Start by cutting off the root and stem ends until you see predominantly ivory flesh. Set the knob on a cutting board and cut down around the curve of the bulb to remove the skin, cutting deeply enough to get rid of most brown spots. Use a paring knife to cut out any spots you missed.
• Like apples or potatoes, celery root browns quickly once cut. You can prevent discoloration by dropping the peeled bulbs in water to which you've added a bit of lemon juice or by tossing the cut root in vinaigrette or a little lemon juice or vinegar.
• Raw celery root is crisp with an intense flavor that is somewhat like a combination of parsley and celery. Use it shredded, or cut into matchsticks in salads or slaws.
• Cooked, the root takes on a milder, satisfyingly nutty flavor and becomes lusciously silky in texture. It's a classic to pair with potatoes—the potatoes' starch content helps to bind the puree, and celery root's flavor adds wonderful depth.
• The root is fabulous roasted. Its flavor is quite strong, making it a good vegetable to roast with a medley of other root vegetables.

⇥ GOOD FOR YOU

In its cooked form, celery root is often compared to potatoes. Unlike potatoes, however, it's a 0 SmartPoints food, so consider using it as a substitute where you can. Celery root is a good source of vitamin C, potassium, and phosphorus.

CHILE PEPPERS

Nothing beats a peck of piquant peppers for spicy variety. They've been cultivated for more than 6,000 years, adding zing and fire to cuisines around the world. Some chiles are so hot they'll knock your socks off, while others can be downright tame. In general, the smaller and narrower the pepper, the more incendiary it will be.

IN SEASON
Year-round

➻CHOOSING & STORING

• Fresh chiles should be firm with tight, glossy or waxy skin that shows no sign of soft spots.
• Refrigerate chiles in a plastic bag up to 1 week.
• The Scoville Scale, named for the scientist who first measured chiles' blazing effect, ranks peppers by their firepower. But it's not absolute; seed lineage, climate, and soil all affect capsaicin, the compound that gives chiles their kick. Despite those variations, use the following as a general guide to heat levels of some common chiles:
Mild: Anaheim, banana
Mild to moderate: poblano, shishito
Moderate: jalapeño
Hot: Serrano, Thai (bird's eye)
Scorching: habanero, Scotch bonnet

➻USE 'EM UP!

• Cutting into a chile releases capsaicin-filled oils, so be extremely careful not to touch your eyes, nose, or mouth—even after washing your hands, because soap won't remove all the residue. In fact, we recommend wearing gloves when preparing fresh chiles.
• To temper some of a pepper's heat, remove the seeds and the fibrous white ribs, which have the highest concentration of capsaicin.
• Chiles' major culinary job is adding spice and depth to other ingredients, although in a few dishes they actually become the stars. Try stuffing large mild or moderate peppers like poblanos and jalapeños with grains, cheese, or ground meat. Or wok-char peppers like shishitos or Anaheims (seeds and all!) and sprinkle them with sea salt.
• Mouth on fire? Try a spoonful of thick dairy like sour cream or yogurt—they're most effective at dissolving the capsaicin. Counterintuitive as it may seem, water will only feed the flames.

➻GOOD FOR YOU

Laboratory studies have shown that capsaicin, the compound that provides chiles with their fiery kick, may be effective in fighting cancer.

COLLARD GREENS

Big flavor, big texture, and big nutrition—collards have a lot to offer! They're one of the South's staple vegetables and are quickly becoming a favorite nationwide. Cook them long and slow (for hours even) until they practically melt, or give them shorter, quicker heat to retain more of their original color and texture—the choice is yours.

IN SEASON
December to April

▸▸ CHOOSING & STORING

• Look for crisp, dark green to blue-green leaves with no sign of wilting or browning.
• Take a pass on leaves with holes or rough edges, both of which can be a sign of insect damage.
• Choose bunches with thinner stalks and small ribs if you can; thick stalks and ribs will have to be stripped out and discarded before cooking, so you won't be eating everything you paid for.
• Store collards in a loosely closed plastic bag in the coldest part of your refrigerator for no more than a few days.
• Collards shrink dramatically during cooking, so you'll need about ⅓ pound fresh greens to yield a ½-cup serving of cooked greens.

▸▸ USE 'EM UP!

• Collards are one of the sturdiest greens; you can steam, braise, or sauté them for minutes or hours. If you're new to collard cooking, you may want to stop and taste them every 5 or 10 minutes to find the texture you like best.
• Collards have lots of flavor on their own, but some tasty additions include garlic, onion, red pepper, cider vinegar, and hot sauce. They're also a natural to stew with bacon or pork.
• Substitute collards for other sturdy greens like kale, Swiss chard, or mustard greens, but remember that collards may require slightly more cooking time.
• Blanched collard leaves are excellent for wrapping up other ingredients. You can use them as a 0 SmartPoints alternative to grain wraps or in place of cabbage leaves or grape leaves.

▸▸ GOOD FOR YOU

Collards are an excellent source of folate and vitamin K.

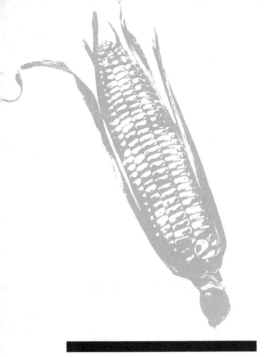

CORN

A North American original, corn is one of the world's most widely grown crops, along with wheat and rice. Sweet corn, of course, is the variety we cook as a vegetable (though it's technically a grain), and corn on the cob routinely tops lists of Americans' all-time favorite vegetables. And baby corn, in case you ever wondered, is truly corn taken off the stalk when tiny and tender.

IN SEASON
July to September

⇥ CHOOSING & STORING

Buying the freshest corn on the cob will really pay off. Its sugars begin to turn to starch the moment it is picked, leaving once delectably sweet, tender kernels dense and tasteless within a few days. Buy corn from a farmers' market or vegetable stand if possible; it's likely to have been picked that day.
• Look for ears snugly wrapped in moist (not dried out) bright green husks. The silk at the tip of the ear should be golden brown; it should look fresh and glossy, not wilted or brittle.
• Peel back the very tip of the husk if you can; look for plump, shiny kernels that are packed along the ear in neat rows. Mushy or discolored kernels may be signs of age or poor handling.
• Refrigerate corn loosely wrapped in a plastic or paper bag no more than 1 day; leaving it in the husk until cooking will help preserve freshness.

⇥ USE 'EM UP!

• **Boil it:** Choose a pot large enough to hold the number of ears you're cooking plus enough water to cover them all by at least 2 inches. Bring the water to a rolling boil, add the corn, cover, and cook until the kernels brighten and plump slightly and are just tender, 1 to 6 minutes after the water comes back to a boil. Drain and serve.
• **Grill it:** Pull down but do not break off the husks and remove the silk. Smooth the husks back over the ear, tie the top with a piece of kitchen string, and soak in cold water for 30 minutes. Grill over medium heat until the kernels are softened and the husks are slightly charred, 10 to 20 minutes. Alternatively, you can brush husked ears with oil (or mayonnaise!), and grill over medium-low heat until very lightly charred.
• **Try it raw:** Very fresh, very sweet corn is excellent raw in salads, slaws, and salsas. To remove kernels from a husked ear, slice off the stem end so that the ear stands level; then hold the tip with one hand and use a knife to cut downward on the ear, removing 3 or 4 rows of kernels with each cut.

⇥ GOOD FOR YOU

In addition to B vitamins, sweet corn is a terrific source of phosphorous. Corn does have a SmartPoints value. A medium ear or ⅔ cup of kernels has a SmartPoints value of 3. Baby corn, however, is a 0 SmartPoints food.

CUCUMBERS

Garden, or slicing, cucumbers are what you're most likely to see stacked at your supermarket. Their thick skins are sometimes bitter and usually coated with a layer of wax, making peeling them mandatory. Preferable in the summer months are smaller, crunchier Kirby, or pickling, cucumbers with bumpy skins and sweet flesh. Also look for English and Persian varieties as year-round alternatives.

⤠ CHOOSING & STORING

Be picky when it comes to cucumbers; bad ones are bitter, watery, and not worth buying.

• Inspect a cucumber's skin to make sure it's firm, unblemished, and taut, not wrinkled. Check the ends for yellowing, a sign of overmaturity.

• Select smaller, thinner specimens of any variety you're buying, and you'll usually be rewarded with superior flavor and crisper texture.

• Cucumbers dehydrate quickly, so refrigerate them no more than a few days in a loosely sealed plastic bag.

• Superlong English, or hothouse, cucumbers are conveniently thin-skinned and virtually seedless; their consistent year-round quality makes them a good choice in the off-season. Less common but also a good choice out of season are petite beauties variously known as Persian, Lebanese, or Middle Eastern cucumbers; these small, thin, dark green cukes are sweet and juicy.

⤠ USE 'EM UP!

How to prepare cucumbers is partly a matter of taste or recipe and partly a matter of variety. Here are some guidelines:

• Always peel the tough, bitter, and often waxed skin of garden cucumbers.

• Soups will be smoother if you use peeled cucumbers, but you may miss the skin's green color in the finished product; use varieties with thin, sweet skins, and you can compromise by leaving the skin on half the amount called for.

• The skins of hothouse and Lebanese cucumbers are thin and delicious, and look particularly attractive with this trick: Run a dinner fork down the length of the cucumber, pressing so that the tines just stripe the surface; continue all around the cucumber, and then slice or cut it as desired.

• Cucumber seeds become larger and more bitter with age; do a taste test to see if the ones in your cucumber should be removed.

• Seed cucumbers by splitting them in half lengthwise and scraping a teaspoon down the center of each half.

⤠ GOOD FOR YOU

Cucumbers are a good source of vitamin K, essential for bone health and proper blood clotting.

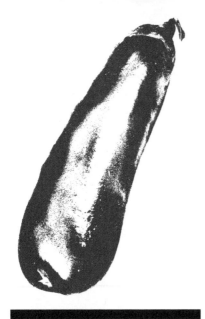

EGGPLANT

Eggplant turns famously rich and meaty with cooking, making it a favorite vegetable across the globe and particularly beloved of vegetarians. Hundreds of varieties are grown worldwide, although by far the most common in the United States is the large deep purple Italian eggplant. Smaller varieties also abound, including slender Japanese, or Asian, eggplant, Thai eggplant, white eggplant, and baby eggplant.

IN SEASON
July to October

↠CHOOSING & STORING

Despite much talk, there is no such thing as "male" or "female" eggplants because all eggplants are self-pollinating. A body of lore suggests that females are more likely to be seedy and bitter, but both of these characteristics are the result of variety and overmaturity, not gender. Concentrate on selecting young, fresh eggplants, and you're likely to be happy with their flavor.
• Look for eggplants with taut, glossy skin without brown spots or indentations. Check the stem; the green cap should be free of mold or brown coloring.
• Pick up each eggplant; heaviness for its size is a sign that the flesh is moist and dense, not dry and seedy (and possibly bitter).
• Store eggplants unwrapped in a cool, dry place or wrapped loosely in plastic in the warmest part of the refrigerator. Fresher is always better with eggplants, so use them within 2 or 3 days.

↠USE 'EM UP!

• Salting was once considered mandatory to remove bitter juices from eggplant, but you're unlikely to find a bitter specimen these days unless it's past its prime. Salting pulls out some moisture and reduces the sponginess of the flesh, resulting in less oil absorption and perhaps better texture after cooking. Can you skip the salting step? The answer is generally yes; reducing the amount of oil in which the eggplant is cooked is a better way to decrease fat absorption.
• There's just about no wrong way to cook eggplant. It's a favorite roasted, braised, stuffed and baked, grilled, stir-fried, pureed, and more.
• Most eggplant varieties have similar flavor and cooking qualities, making experimentation easy.
• Unless you actually burn it, it's difficult to overcook eggplant—another thing to love about this vegetable. The longer it cooks, the more flavorful and silky in texture it becomes.
• Take advantage of eggplant's meaty flavor and texture by replacing half the meat in chilies, stews, or Bolognese sauce with diced eggplant.

↠GOOD FOR YOU

Eggplant contains a good amount of fiber and the antioxidant nasunin, both concentrated in the vegetable's skin.

ENDIVE

Lovely, versatile endive, a.k.a. Belgian endive, has been cultivated only since the 1830s, making it a relative newcomer to the vegetable market. Most Americans know it as a crunchy, pleasantly bitter addition to salads, while Europeans are more likely to cook it until it turns sweet and tender. Escarole, sometimes called endive, and frisée are also members of Belgium endive's chicory family but are treated in this book as lettuces (see page 55).

⇥ CHOOSING & STORING

• Choose densely packed solid heads of absolutely crisp leaves.
• Endive will turn green and bitter when exposed to light, which is why the heads are often wrapped in tissue. If yours aren't, you can wrap them in a paper towel before placing them in a loosely sealed plastic bag.
• Keep endive in the crisper drawer of your refrigerator and it should stay sweet and crunchy for 1 to 2 weeks.
• Only the very outer leaves on the head need to be rinsed before serving.
• The classic endive variety, sometimes known as white Belgian endive, is a pale beauty with glossy white leaves tipped in greenish yellow. Look also for California, or red, endive, a cross between Belgian endive and radicchio di Treviso that features scarlet-red tips and a slightly more pungent flavor.

⇥ USE 'EM UP!

• Not a fan of endive's bitterness? The vegetable's pungency is concentrated towards the base of the leaves and in the head's core; removing these parts will lessen its bite if you're serving it raw. Cooking also neutralizes its bitterness, leaving it mild and quite sweet.
• Using red endive raw is preferred as it will lose its distinctive scarlet hue with cooking.
• Don't use a cast-iron pan to cook endive or it may turn an unappealing gray color.
• Just about anything you can spread on a cracker you can spoon into raw endive leaves: dips, soft cheeses, seafood salads, salsas, and more.

⇥ GOOD FOR YOU

Belgian endive is an excellent source of vitamin K and a good source of vitamin A.

FENNEL

Fennel's thick, crisp, bunching stems may remind you of celery, and the two are quite closely related: Both are members of the aromatic Apiaceae family, which also includes anise, parsley, and dill. Fennel's strong licorice-like flavor and extreme crunch make it a favorite for eating raw, albeit usually sliced thin so it plays well with other ingredients. Cooked it becomes nutty and buttery with a seductive hint of anise.

➤➤ CHOOSING & STORING
• Look for pure white bulbs topped by abundant dark green fronds that show no sign of wilting.
• Select smaller bulbs for salads and other raw uses as they are milder and slightly more tender.
• Choose larger bulbs for cooking; they halve or quarter more easily, and their stronger flavor and denser texture will be mellowed with heat.
• Store fennel loosely in a plastic bag in the refrigerator crisper 3 to 4 days.

➤➤ USE 'EM UP!
• Raw fennel adds outstanding crunch and flavor to salads, slaws, and salsas. Try it in tuna salad, Waldorf salad, or anywhere else you would use raw celery, but remember that its flavor is quite assertive.
• Cooked fennel is sweet, mild, and meltingly tender. Halve or quarter bulbs, and grill, roast, steam, or braise; dice or thinly slice and add to soups, stews, or sautés.
• However you enjoy it, do save fennel's feathery fronds when you trim a bulb: They make a superb garnish reminiscent of dill.
• Fennel will begin to brown an hour or so after being cut; toss it with lemon juice or an acidic dressing to keep it white.
• Fennel goes brilliantly with the flavors of citrus, apple, tomato, anchovies, olives, almonds, walnuts, tangy cheeses, seafood, and wine.

➤➤ GOOD FOR YOU
Fennel is a great vegetable source of vitamin C. One 8-ounce bulb contains 28 mg, almost half the recommended daily dose.

GREEN BEANS

You may have heard green beans called "string beans," a holdover from the days when most varieties had a tough, fibrous string running the length of the pod. Today the majority are bred to be stringless, so removing this fiber ("stringing") is a thing of the past: Most varieties require just a nipping of the stem end. In addition to green beans, look for pale yellow wax beans, which are almost identical in taste and cooking qualities.

▸▸ CHOOSING & STORING
• Very fresh beans will be straight, smooth, and vibrantly colored and show no signs of wrinkling. The tips of the beans should look sprightly, not browned or limp.
• Select crisp beans that snap rather than bend.
• Green beans should smell fresh and faintly grassy; those with no aroma at all may be past their prime.
• If you see bumps where the bean's seeds lie in the pod, the bean is overmature and will be tough and bland, not tender and sweet.
• Purple green beans are sometimes available, particularly at farmers' markets, but be aware that they turn green with cooking. Also look out for slim, tender haricots verts, a delicate and delicious variety that needs just a minute or two of steaming or boiling.
• Refrigerate green beans in a paper bag or loosely closed plastic bag 2 to 3 days.

▸▸ USE 'EM UP!
• Add a pinch of sugar to the cooking water to sweeten beans, particularly those that might be a little past their prime.
• Green beans are excellent on a crudités platter. For best color and flavor, blanch the beans by cooking them in a large pot of boiling water for 30 seconds, draining, and immediately cooling them in cold water.
• Acidic ingredients like vinegar or lemon juice will turn beans from bright green to dull khaki. The color change won't affect the beans' flavor, but if you want them to keep their vibrant color, add acids or vinaigrettes just before serving.
• Green beans go particularly well with citrus, nuts, fennel, tomatoes, onions, garlic, ginger, olives, feta, Parmesan, soy sauce, and cumin.

▸▸ GOOD FOR YOU
One cup of cooked green beans delivers a hearty 4 g of fiber.

JICAMA

Peel off this tuber's plain brown wrapper and you're in for a treat: crisp, juicy, pure white flesh with a delightfully sweet flavor and excellent crunch. Almost all jicama is grown in Mexico, where it is traditionally served raw —sometimes accompanied by chili powder, lime, and salt to accentuate its mild flavor. Jicama can also be cooked: it maintains crunch and sweetness well in dishes like stir-fries, soups, and stews.

↦ CHOOSING & STORING
• Choose jicama with smooth, thin, unblemished skins; a slight shine is an indication of freshness.
• Select small- or medium-size tubers; very large ones are often woody and bland.
• Refrigerate jicama in a paper bag—never in plastic—up to 2 weeks.

↦ USE 'EM UP!
• A paring knife or vegetable peeler is ideal for removing jicama's brown skin; if there's a tough, fibrous layer under the skin, be sure to remove that as well.
• Grate jicama to add to slaws, salsas, sandwiches, and tacos.
• Slice jicama into matchsticks or batons to use in summer rolls, stir-fries, and salads or almost any place you might use raw carrots.
• Diced jicama is excellent steamed or sautéed with other vegetables or added to soups, curries, or stews.
• Serve chunks of raw jicama with tropical fruits like pineapple, mango, and papaya.
• Cut jicama into spears or rounds to serve with dips and dressings, or just sprinkle with lime juice and chili powder for a piquant snack.

↦ GOOD FOR YOU
Jicama is packed with vitamin C and is an excellent source of fiber.

KALE

Not only is this sturdy cold-weather green packed with flavor and character, it also holds the distinction of being one of the most nutrient-dense vegetables. Ruffled curly kale can be green or purple and has a toothsome texture and a mild, cabbage-like flavor. Very dark, slender-leafed Tuscan kale (a.k.a. Lacinato kale, dinosaur kale, or cavolo nero) has a particularly rich, earthy flavor and meltingly tender texture when cooked.

➡ CHOOSING & STORING

• Select bunches with medium or small leaves with tender-looking stems and ribs; very large stems and ribs will have to be discarded, meaning more work and more waste.
• Avoid kale with dried-out or yellowed leaves, both a sign of age or poor storage. Leaves with holes in them may mean the plant has been damaged by insects.
• Kale keeps best at low temperatures, so store it in the coldest part of your refrigerator, sealed in a plastic bag, no more than 2 days.
• Conventionally grown kale may have a high pesticide residue, so consider buying organic.
• Kale is usually available year-round, but it's sweeter when harvested after the first frost.

➡ USE 'EM UP!

• A standard bunch of kale weighs about ¾ pound. It will yield about 10 lightly packed cups when trimmed and coarsely chopped.
• Clean kale by first discarding any yellowed or damaged leaves and then rinsing the bunch very well. Cut off any tough stems from the leaves; if the ribs are thick and tough looking, strip out the ribs with your hands.
• Slice kale leaves very thinly and add raw to salads and slaws.
• Steam kale by combining it in a large skillet with a few tablespoons of water or broth; cover and cook until it reaches the desired tenderness.
• Chop kale and add it to soups, stews, pastas, and casseroles.
• Roast large pieces of kale leaves tossed with a little oil and salt until crisped for wonderfully crunchy kale "chips."
• Kale is richly flavored on its own, but also pairs well with the strong flavors of soy sauce, chile peppers, onions, garlic, ginger, bacon, vinegar, olives, and feta and Parmesan cheeses.

➡ GOOD FOR YOU

Kale is a nutritional powerhouse. A cooked 1-cup serving provides more than the recommended daily dose of vitamin A and is packed with vitamin K. It's also an excellent source of a number of antioxidants that may protect the body from chronic diseases.

LETTUCE

It's difficult to imagine a culinary world without lettuces. Soft or crunchy, mild or bittersweet, palest yellow to deepest purple —these miraculous greens add beauty, depth, and outstanding nutrition to our everyday meals. We think first and foremost of a crisp, raw salad when we think of lettuce, but many varieties are well suited to short cooking in either braises or soups.

⇢CHOOSING & STORING

- Inspect lettuce leaves and heads carefully and reject any that have brown, wilted, or slimy leaves.
- Give lettuce the sniff test: It should smell fresh and grassy, not sour or very earthy.
- Wrap lettuce in a paper towel (this will absorb excess moisture, the enemy of greens' freshness) and then place in a sealed plastic bag in the crisper drawer of your refrigerator.
- If greens are wilted from summer heat or improper handling, they may revive if soaked in very cold water for a few minutes, spun until bone-dry in a salad spinner, and then wrapped and refrigerated for an hour or two.
- Lettuce is a crop that typically has high pesticide residue when conventionally grown, so buy organic when possible.
- Rinse lettuce well before using; dirt and sand can hide in the folds of leaves and give you a gritty salad. Rinsing also helps reduce illness-causing bacteria that may be present and removes some of the pesticide residue that clings to conventionally grown greens.

⇢USE 'EM UP!

- To clean leaf lettuce, fill a sink or large bowl with cold water and submerge leaves completely. Swish the leaves around with your hands and then let them soak for a few minute to allow grit to sink to the bottom. Scoop leaves up and drain.
- An alternate method is to rinse each leaf individually under cold running water and then drain; this is time-consuming but may work better if you have sink or space issues.
- Iceberg lettuce is an exception; to clean this dense head you need only remove and discard the outer leaves and then rinse the base.
- A salad spinner is excellent for removing moisture from lettuce. If you don't have one, place damp leaves in a single layer on a kitchen towel or double layer of paper towels, roll everything up loosely, and give the roll a few bounces.
- Cut or tear salad greens and dress as close to serving time as possible for best flavor and texture.

⇢GOOD FOR YOU

Although nutrient content varies from variety to variety, you can count on most types of lettuce for vitamins A, C, and K as well as folate and fiber.

green leaf

Loose heads of tender, rounded, light-green leaves; mild flavor

BEST FOR:
Salads, lettuce wraps, lining bowls and platters

GOOD TO KNOW:
A top choice for wraps

bibb

Very small heads of soft, loosely curled leaves; buttery, fresh flavor

BEST FOR:
Salads, lettuce cups, braising whole heads

GOOD TO KNOW:
A member of the butterhead family; smaller than but generally interchangeable with more common Boston

radicchio

Small, tightly packed heads of white-veined maroon leaves; lightly bitter flavor

BEST FOR:
Salads, braising, grilling, lining bowls and platters

GOOD TO KNOW:
Actually a member of the endive family

boston

Small, loose heads of tender, ruffled leaves; buttery, mineral flavor

BEST FOR:
Salads, lettuce wraps, braising whole heads, lining bowls and platters

GOOD TO KNOW:
A member of the butterhead family; bruises easily so handle and rinse very gently

mesclun

Mixture of young lettuce and other salad leaves, usually in contrasting colors and shapes

BEST FOR:
Salads, garnish

GOOD TO KNOW:
Choose carefully; mesclun mixes at their best are fresh, flavorful, and delightful, but they can also be tired, bland, and even sour

lollo rosso

Loose heads of ruffled, tender leaves that are light green with brilliant purplish-red edges

BEST FOR:
Salads, lettuce wraps, lining bowls and platters

GOOD TO KNOW:
Prized for its attractive color contrast

red oak

Loose heads of thin, notched, maroon to purple leaves; buttery, mild mineral flavor

BEST FOR:
Salads, lining bowls and platters

GOOD TO KNOW:
Very attractive when mixed with pale-green leaves

watercress

Tender sprigs of round, jade-green leaves; sprightly, fresh, lightly tangy flavor

BEST FOR:
Salads, sandwiches, soups, garnish

GOOD TO KNOW:
Actually a member of the cabbage family

romaine

Very tall, closely packed heads of crisp, dark green to light green leaves; sweet to bittersweet, mild mineral flavor

BEST FOR:
Salads, shredding, braising, grilling

GOOD TO KNOW:
Also known as Cos lettuce; crisp enough to substitute for iceberg lettuce in most dishes

frisée

Small heads of thin, frilly, very crisp leaves; bittersweet flavor

BEST FOR:
Salads, garnish

GOOD TO KNOW:
Actually a member of the endive family

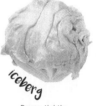

iceberg

Dense, tightly packed heads of extremely crisp light-green leaves; refreshing and very mildly flavored

BEST FOR:
Salads, shredding, wedging

GOOD TO KNOW:
A high water content makes it the crispest of all lettuces; use for textural contrast

escarole

Broad, frilled leaves with creamy yellow to dark green coloring; fresh, mildly bitter flavor

BEST FOR:
Use the lighter, inner leaves for salads, or braise or sauté the whole head

GOOD TO KNOW:
Actually a member of the endive family

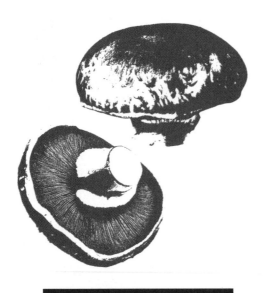

MUSHROOMS

Venture beyond the common white button mushroom, and you'll enter an intriguing and rewarding world of hundreds of delicious varieties. Adding to mushrooms' mystery is the fact that they aren't really vegetables at all, but fungi that grow and reproduce without the benefit of roots, leaves, seeds, or flowers.

IN SEASON
Year-round

↠CHOOSING & STORING

Characteristics vary widely from variety to variety, but here are some general tips:
• Mushrooms should be springy and somewhat dense in texture; avoid any that are limp, slimy, or dried out. Caps should be smooth and free of cracks, breaks, or nibble marks, and stems should be free of holes, a sign of insect damage.
• Mushrooms should have a pleasant earthy aroma; any that smell musty or sour will probably taste that way.
• Refrigerate mushrooms in the box they came in or in a paper bag. Store them away from moisture on a refrigerator shelf, not in a vegetable drawer.
• Until recently, most mushroom varieties resisted cultivation, making them local specialties available only to foragers or restaurateurs willing to pay top dollar. New growing techniques have expanded the number of varieties commercially available; even those commonly labeled "wild" at your market were probably harvested by specialty growers.
• Dried porcini, morels, and other varieties are handy for adding concentrated mushroom flavor to dishes. Reconstitute them in hot water for about 20 minutes.

↠USE 'EM UP!

• Use a soft brush or damp paper towel to remove any loose dirt from mushroom caps and stems.
• Avoid rinsing mushrooms unless they are very dirty, and never soak them: Mushrooms absorb water quickly, becoming soggy and unappealing.
• Trim off woody stems, tough bases, or any discolored areas with a paring knife; you can save the scraps to flavor soups or stocks.
• Only a few varieties, including white mushrooms, cremini and enokis, are suitable for eating raw; others will be musty or tough if left uncooked.
• Sautéing is one of the best ways to concentrate the flavor of mushrooms and enjoy them in everything from omelets to soups to pastas.
• Mushrooms are superb grilled. Larger varieties such as portobellos can be grilled like burgers.

↠GOOD FOR YOU

Mushrooms contain significant amounts of phosphorous and niacin, as well as being one of the few food sources of vitamin D.

porcini

Bulbous beige or ivory stems topped with golden-brown caps; rich, smoky flavor and deep, woodsy aroma

BEST FOR:
Sautéing, roasting, soups

GOOD TO KNOW:
Dried porcini are readily available and flavorful but lack the creamy, meaty texture prized in the fresh mushrooms

chanterelle

Bright yellow to orange with a frilled, trumpet-like shape; rich, buttery, and earthy flavor

BEST FOR:
Sautéing, roasting, soups

GOOD TO KNOW:
A favorite for its distinctive coloring and deep flavor

morel

Thick, tube-like stems with a honeycombed cap; very intense smoky, nutty, earthy flavor

BEST FOR:
Sautéing, roasting, soups

GOOD TO KNOW:
Prized for its strong flavor and sponge-like ability to absorb other flavors

white

Firm, thick white caps and squat stems; very mild woodsy flavor

BEST FOR:
Eating raw, sautéing, roasting, grilling, soups

GOOD TO KNOW:
Good all-purpose mushroom for everything from salads to kebabs to stuffing

hen-of-the-woods

Large brown to beige, leafy clusters; very meaty; rich, spicy flavor

BEST FOR:
Sautéing, roasting

GOOD TO KNOW:
Also known as maitake, these tree mushrooms are superb for roasting

black trumpet

Delicate trumpet shape; slightly chewy with deep, earthy flavor

BEST FOR:
Sautéing, steaming, soups

GOOD TO KNOW:
Strong flavor and dramatic appearance make them a chef favorite

oyster

Brown to gray to yellow with soft, velvety stems and caps; sweet, delicate flavor

BEST FOR:
Sautéing, steaming, roasting, soups

GOOD TO KNOW:
Excellent for stir-fries and quick sautés

cremini

Dark brown, squat, and meaty; smoky, lightly nutty in flavor

BEST FOR:
Eating raw, sautéing, steaming, roasting, grilling, soups

GOOD TO KNOW:
Young portobello mushroom, sometimes called "baby bella"; a flavorful all-purpose mushroom

enoki

Small ivory caps with very long, slender stems; sweet and earthy with pronounced crunch

BEST FOR:
Eating raw, sautéing, steaming, soups

GOOD TO KNOW:
Preserve enokis' distinctive crisp texture by eating them raw or with very brief cooking

bluefoot

Beige caps and stems with hints of lavender; meaty and lightly earthy

BEST FOR:
Sautéing, roasting, soups

GOOD TO KNOW:
Also known as blewits

shiitake

Very tough stems topped with dark-brown, flexible caps; rich, meaty flavor

BEST FOR:
Sautéing, steaming, grilling, soups

GOOD TO KNOW:
Although edible, the stems are so fibrous that they are rarely eaten

portobello

Huge brown caps with brown to black gills; deep earthy, lightly sweet and oaky flavor

BEST FOR:
Sautéing, roasting, grilling

GOOD TO KNOW:
These oversized caps are excellent for stuffing or grilling and slicing

ONIONS

Who could imagine cooking without onions? This venerable vegetable has a long, storied history stretching back so far that even experts disagree on its culinary origins. Today onions find their way into almost every kind of savory dish in almost every land, from soups and stews to curries and stir-fries, and, of course, in salads of every stripe. Onions are loosely classified as either dry, or "storage," onions, with papery skin, or fresh, young "green onions."

⇢ CHOOSING & STORING

• Look for onions with tight, dry, papery skins; shiny onions stripped of their fragile skins will not store well. Avoid onions with green sprouts, a sign of age or incorrect storage.
• Onions store best in a basket kept in a cool, dark place; do not refrigerate onions.
• If buying green onions (scallions, spring onions, or leeks), look for glossy white bulbs and sprightly green tops. Store green onions in a plastic bag in the coldest part of the refrigerator up to 1 week.

⇢ USE 'EM UP!

• Onions have volatile sulfur compounds that are released into the air when their cell walls are cut. These compounds reduce some cooks to tears, while others can cut onion after onion with barely a sniff. Try these tricks if you're in the former category:

Refrigerate onions for 30 minutes before cutting to help minimize the release of sulfur.

Make sure your knife is very sharp—a honed blade will cut through the cell walls neatly, releasing less sulfur.

Turn on your kitchen exhaust fan and chop on a cutting board set directly underneath the fan.

Wear a pair of safety goggles while you chop. Good news for contact lens wearers: Contacts actually provide a level of protection against onion fumes and their irritation.

• Choose sweet onion varieties like Vidalia, Walla Walla, or Maui for serving raw in salads, sandwiches, tacos, and in rings on burgers. You can also tame pungent varieties by slicing them and soaking them in ice water 30 minutes, draining them, and blotting them dry.

• You can store onion skins and ends and the trimmings from scallions and leeks in a zip-close plastic bag in the freezer, and then use them next time you make a stock or broth or to infuse milk with onion flavor for a sauce.

⇢ GOOD FOR YOU

Onions contain modest amounts of vitamin C plus a good dose of fiber. But it's their combination of flavonoids and sulfur-containing compounds that have led researchers to believe they may have cardiovascular and anticancer benefits.

baby

Very small, with mild to moderate bite and earthy flavor

BEST FOR:
Roasting, braising, pickling

GOOD TO KNOW:
Also known as pickling or boiling onions; can be any variety of early-harvested, immature onion

cipollini

Small, disc-shaped, with rich, sweet, earthy flavor and mild bite

BEST FOR:
Roasting, braising, pickling

GOOD TO KNOW:
Prized for their complex flavor and unusual button-like shape

maui

Large, crisp, very sweet and mild

BEST FOR:
Slicing, salads, grilling

GOOD TO KNOW:
In season April to July

leek

Thick white stalk and broad dark-green leaves with a sweet, fresh, and mild onion flavor

BEST FOR:
Roasting, braising, soups

GOOD TO KNOW:
Fibrous when raw but meltingly tender with cooking

spanish

Large, fairly mild and juicy

BEST FOR:
Salads, sautéing, caramelizing, soups, grilling, roasting

GOOD TO KNOW:
A good choice for both eating raw and cooking

red

Medium to large, deep purple or magenta, and very crisp with mild to moderate bite

BEST FOR:
Slicing, salads, grilling, roasting

GOOD TO KNOW:
A very versatile onion: an excellent flavor and color addition to salads, plus firm texture and good flavor balance for cooking

pearl

Very small, very mild onion about the size of a large marble

BEST FOR:
Roasting, braising, pickling, garnishing

GOOD TO KNOW:
Peeling these minis can be time consuming, making them a popular onion to buy frozen and pan ready

scallion

Slender white base and long green leaves with mild onion flavor

BEST FOR:
Slicing, salads, stir-fries, garnish, grilling, soups

GOOD TO KNOW:
Also known as green onions

texas sweet

Large, crisp, very sweet

BEST FOR:
Slicing, salads, grilling, baking

GOOD TO KNOW:
In season March to April

white

Tangy, pungent and very crisp

BEST FOR:
Sautéing, roasting, baking

GOOD TO KNOW:
A good all-purpose cooking onion

spring onion

Small to medium snow white onions with abundant greenery on top; fresh tasting with balanced sweet-pungent flavor

BEST FOR:
Slicing, salads, roasting, braising, soups

GOOD TO KNOW:
Use the green tops as well as the white bulbs

vidalia

Large, crisp, juicy, very sweet and mild

BEST FOR: Slicing, salads, grilling

GOOD TO KNOW:
In season April to June

walla walla

Large, crisp, very sweet and mild

BEST FOR:
Slicing, salads, grilling

GOOD TO KNOW:
In season June to August

yellow

Juicy, pungent

BEST FOR:
Sautéing, roasting, baking

GOOD TO KNOW:
A good all-purpose cooking onion

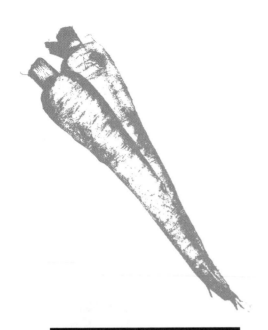

▸▸CHOOSING & STORING

- The freshest parsnips will have smooth, creamy-beige skin and be very firm. Flabby, wrinkled parsnips may be all you'll find out of season; older roots loose sweetness and may have a woody or hollow interior.
- Parsnips come in a variety of shapes, from long and tapering to very slender to quite thick and stout. Choose ones as uniform as possible so your preparation is easier and cooking times remain consistent. Twisted or bumpy roots will be a little more difficult to peel but their quality should not be compromised.
- Refrigerate parsnips loosely wrapped in a paper towel and then in a plastic bag for 1 to 2 weeks.

▸▸USE 'EM UP!

- Parsnip skin is usually tough, and often a bit dirty, so peeling is always recommended and is just as easy as peeling carrots.
- Parsnips are a fabulous addition to roast root vegetable medleys, where they caramelize easily and become wonderfully sweet and nutty.
- Add chunks of parsnip to stews or casseroles. They can also be made into a delicious puree, but one that tends to be watery: Stir the puree over medium-low heat to allow excess moisture to evaporate. A combination of half pureed parsnips, half potatoes makes a terrific alternative to the usual mash.
- Parsnips' light anise flavor pairs well with the rich dairy and cheeses in gratins, casseroles, and purees. It also combines wonderfully with strongly flavored ingredients like onions, garlic, tart apples, nutmeg, cumin, curry, cayenne, and bacon.

▸▸GOOD FOR YOU

Parsnips are rich in potassium, folic acid, and vitamin C. They are one of the few vegetables that have a SmartPoints value: half a medium raw parsnip or ½ cup chopped raw or cooked parsnip has a SmartPoints value of 2.

PARSNIPS

While the parsnip's slender shape and crisp texture show its close relation to carrots, its sweet, lightly anise-like flavor hints at its affiliation to celery root. And while these ivory-colored roots are sometimes slightly gnarly and twisted, they're as easy to prepare as any root vegetable and wonderfully unexpected: Add them to soups, stews, or roast vegetables in place of potatoes or carrots.

PEAS

Peas belong to the legume family, but unlike legumes such as lentils and beans, they are most often eaten fresh, not dried. Green peas, sometimes called English peas, have a short season in spring and early summer. If you can get them absolutely fresh, they are a revelation. Snap and snow peas boast pods that are tender enough to eat. They're prized for their sweetness and fresh, grassy flavor, and can be eaten either cooked or, if very fresh, raw.

IN SEASON
May to July

↦ CHOOSING & STORING
- Freshness is paramount in the pea family. Look for vibrant green shells with evidence of plump, evenly packed seeds inside. The tastiest peas will be moderately sized, not overly large.
- Look for snow peas with a few green petals at the stem end; this is a sign of freshness and proper handling.
- Snap peas should be supercrisp and, true to their name, give a good snap when broken in half.
- Taste a sample raw; it should be sweet and crisp with a springlike flavor and only a hint of starch.
- Refrigerate peas for no more than 2 days in either a loosely closed plastic bag or in a paper bag.
- Frozen peas, processed just after harvesting, maintain their integrity quite well and definitely deserve a place in your freezer.

↦ USE 'EM UP!
- The crispness of fresh peas should always shine through. Avoid long cooking; instead, opt for steaming, stir-frying, or blanching.
- To set peas' color for using cold in salads or warm-weather dishes, boil or steam them just until they turn bright green; then immediately cool in cold water. Drain and pat them dry; you can wrap the peas in paper towels, seal in a plastic bag, and refrigerate them up to 2 days.
- Don't forget to try using very fresh peas raw. Snap peas and snow peas can be thinly sliced, and green peas just need shelling.
- Properly cooked peas of all stripes are brilliant with just a little sea salt and a squeeze of lemon. But they also have an affinity for the Asian flavors of soy sauce, ginger, chiles, and coconut. And try them mixed with other classic spring ingredients like asparagus, mild onions, mint, and dill.

↦ GOOD FOR YOU
Green peas, snow peas, and snap peas all have significant amounts of vitamins C and K, magnesium, and fiber. While snow peas and snap peas are 0 SmartPoints foods, green peas are not: ½ cup of steamed or raw green peas clocks in at 2 SmartPoints value.

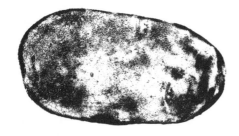

POTATOES

Odd colors, small sizes, and quirky shapes are in when it comes to potatoes. Varieties with offbeat characteristics were once the province of small growers and sold almost exclusively at farmers' markets. Today, however, they're being harvested in increasing numbers and are showing up everywhere. Still, the plain brown russet can also yield a sublime potato experience.

►► CHOOSING & STORING

• Potatoes should feel firm, never rubbery or dried out. Skins should be uniformly colored and free of blotches, cracks, sprouting, or soft spots.
• Avoid potatoes with a green cast to their skin; this is a sign of age or improper storage, and indicates the presence of solanine, a mild toxin.
• Store potatoes in a cool, dark place away from moisture. A basket is ideal for allowing good air circulation, important for maintaining freshness. Properly harvested and stored potatoes should last several weeks.
• Check stored potatoes periodically and remove any that show softening, wrinkling, or sprouting—one bad potato really can spoil the bunch.

►► USE 'EM UP!

Potatoes are broken loosely into three categories based on cooking qualities.
• **Floury varieties** are low in sugar, high in starch, and cook up light and fluffy. Most common in this category are russets, famous for making wonderfully smooth and light mashes, tender roast potatoes, and crispy fries.
• **Waxy potatoes** are lower in starch and higher in sugar, and cook up firm and moist. This makes them ideal for potato salad, and their buttery texture is wonderful for diced roast potatoes. They also make delicious, although moist and dense, mashes.
• **Sweet potatoes**, although similar in growing habits and appearance to regular potatoes, are not closely related. "Yam" is also a misnomer because true yams are tropical tubers with dry, bland flesh. We include them here since their selection and cooking qualities are so similar to those of regular potatoes. They can be cooked virtually any way you can other potatoes, and they also show up in sweet preparations like tasty quick breads and divine pie.

►► GOOD FOR YOU

Potatoes are one of the few vegetables that have a SmartPoints value, so be sure to measure your servings. A small (5-ounce) potato has a SmartPoints value of 3. Half a medium (10-ounce) baked sweet potato has a SmartPoints value of 4.

fingerlings

Small, long, sometimes bumpy potatoes in a variety of skin and flesh colors; generally firm and flavorful

BEST FOR: Steaming, roasting whole, boiling, salads

GOOD TO KNOW: Generally of excellent flavor and texture; best to prepare them in dishes that will highlight their unique shape

new

Any variety of potato harvested when still young and immature

BEST FOR: Steaming, roasting whole or halved, boiling, salads

GOOD TO KNOW: Most, but not all, new potatoes are waxy varieties; red-skinned are the most widely available of this type

russet

Generally large and oblong with rough, brown, sometimes scaly skin; floury flesh that turns light and tender with cooking

BEST FOR: Baking, mashing, frying, casseroles

GOOD TO KNOW: Also known as baking potatoes and Idaho potatoes; a top choice for baking whole and for fluffy mashed potatoes

sweet

Generally large and oblong with red, orange, or beige skin and ivory, yellow, or orange flesh; very sweet, moist, and complexly flavored

BEST FOR: Steaming, roasting, boiling, baking, mashing, frying, casseroles

GOOD TO KNOW: Sometimes incorrectly called a yam

purple

Deep-purple or blue-black skin and purple flesh that turns violet or violet-gray with cooking; texture varies, but is usually dry and floury

BEST FOR: Roasting, boiling, mashing, grating, salads

GOOD TO KNOW: Of ancient origin, but newly popular in today's markets

red-skinned

Deep red to dusty pink skins and white to ivory flesh; texture is firm and waxy

BEST FOR: Steaming, boiling, baking, mashing, salads, casseroles

GOOD TO KNOW: A wonderfully firm and full-flavored choice for classic potato salad

white

Round, small to large, with thin tan skin and bright white flesh; moderately waxy flesh

BEST FOR: Boiling, mashing, casseroles, soups and stews

GOOD TO KNOW: Waxy but still tender texture make it tops for adding to soups and stews

yellow

Round, small to medium potatoes with tan skins and yellow to deep golden flesh; waxy and flavorful when cooked

BEST FOR: Steaming, roasting, boiling, baking, mashing, salads, casseroles

GOOD TO KNOW: Common varieties include Yukon gold and Yellow Finn; both are excellent for mashed potatoes and potato salad

RADISHES

Crisp, pungent, tongue-tingling radishes add color and zing to everything from salads and sandwiches to breakfast plates. Die-hard radish fans even sauté or roast them. The most popular variety for salads and snacking are hot pink or crimson radishes known variously as spring radishes, summer radishes, and table radishes. Look out for other varieties like French breakfast and fanciful watermelon radishes.

IN SEASON
May to June

⇥ CHOOSING & STORING
• Check attached greenery to see that it looks fresh and sprightly.
• Radishes should be very firm and heavy; softness or a light feeling may mean they are pithy and mealy, not crisp, inside.
• Remove green tops and refrigerate radishes in a plastic bag up to 1 week.
• If radish tops are in good shape, fresh and somewhat crisp with no wilting or browning, they can be wrapped in a paper towel and then in a plastic bag and refrigerated for 1 to 2 days. Use these lightly peppery tops as you would arugula.

⇥ USE 'EM UP!
• For added crispness, trim radishes, cover with ice water, and refrigerate 1 to 2 hours.
• Peel radishes if you want a milder flavor; their heat is concentrated near the skin.
• Try cooking with radishes; they're excellent sautéed or stewed with other vegetables, particularly spring vegetables. They can be cooked any way you would cook small turnips.
• Small baby radishes make an excellent addition to spring crudité platters (leave the delicate greens on). Rounds of larger daikon or black radishes can be used as dippers year-round.
• A favorite radish in Asian cuisines is daikon, a huge, juicy, mild root that's good for pickling and for adding a refreshing note to soups or salads. A daikon heirloom known as the watermelon radish combines a pale green exterior ring with a rosy interior and makes a dramatic addition to salads.
• Fresh, sprightly, radish tops can be rinsed well to remove any grit and added to salads, sautéed by themselves or with other greens, used in soups, or pureed in a pesto-like preparation. But give wilted or browned tops a pass—they won't be worth the effort.

⇥ GOOD FOR YOU
One cup of sliced radishes has a full 2 g of dietary fiber and a good part of the recommended daily amount of vitamin C.

SPINACH

Spinach has been celebrated by a diverse group of characters. Florentine native Catherine de Medici is purported to have requested it at every meal, hence the term "Florentine" for spinach-based dishes. And cartoon sailor Popeye ate it to build shirt-popping muscles. Originating in Persia, this high-profile vegetable traveled to China by way of India in the seventh century. Today it's prized world-wide for its versatility and nutrition.

IN SEASON
March through May and September through October

↠ CHOOSING & STORING
• Look for deep green leaves that are firm and crisp. Avoid leaves that are yellowing, bruised, or slimy.
• For salads, choose small tender leaves. Reserve larger leaves with thicker stems for cooking.
• Do not wash spinach before storing. Refrigerate in a perforated plastic bag 3 to 4 days.

↠ USE 'EM UP!
• Because it's grown in sandy soil, spinach needs to be thoroughly rinsed before using. Separate bunched spinach into leaves, trim tough stems, and immerse in a big bowl or sink of water, agitating the leaves to loosen sand clinging to the leaves. Lift the spinach out of the water (the silt should remain at the bottom of the bowl or sink), and repeat washing once or twice more, or until leaves are thoroughly clean.
• Bagged spinach or baby spinach should be fine with a brief rinsing in a colander.
• Avoid using aluminum pans when cooking spinach as it can adversely affect its color and taste.
• Drain spinach thoroughly after cooking to avoid puddles of liquid on your plate or watery recipes.
• One pound of spinach will yield about 10 cups cleaned torn leaves, or when cooked, about 1 to 1⅓ cups (two to three good servings).

↠ GOOD FOR YOU
Spinach is one of the most nutrient-dense foods on the planet. In addition to being rich in vitamins A, C, and K, a cooked cup is a good source of potassium, phosphorous, magnesium, and fiber and contains a number of antioxidants.

TOMATOES

Botanically a fruit but widely accepted as a vegetable, the tomato originated in the Andean regions of South America, eventually finding its way to North America more than 2,000 years ago. Because of their association with the nightshade family, they initially were thought to be poisonous. Yet once the Italians popularized them and the French dubbed them "love apples" (crediting them with aphrodisiac qualities), they became a favored ingredient.

IN SEASON
July to October

⇾ CHOOSING & STORING
• Choose firm—not hard—deeply colored tomatoes that are fragrant and heavy for their size. Avoid tomatoes that are bruised and soft.
• Do not refrigerate whole ripe tomatoes. Store them at room temperature away from sunlight 3 to 4 days.
• If they are unripe, put tomatoes in a paper bag with an apple. The ethylene gas given off by the apple will speed up the ripening process.
• Once cut, tomatoes should be wrapped in plastic and placed in the refrigerator.

⇾ USE 'EM UP!
• Raw tomatoes are almost always eaten with the peel left intact: The peel is a concentrated source of fiber and nutrients; it also helps slices and wedges of tomato hold their shape.
• For some cooked dishes, such as homemade tomato sauce and stews or braises that are simmered for a while, it's advisable to peel tomatoes as heat toughens the skin. To peel, use a sharp knife and cut an X at the base of the tomato. Blanch it in boiling water 20 to 30 seconds, or until the edges of the X begin to curl. Transfer to a bowl of cold water to cool and then slip off the peel.
• To seed tomatoes, simply slice them in half horizontally and use your fingers to scoop out and discard the seeds.
• Got tomatoes with less than stellar flavor? In cooked dishes try adding a pinch of sugar or a bit of balsamic vinegar. A drizzle of balsamic is also a good way to perk up raw tomatoes, as is a pinch of coarse sea salt.

⇾ GOOD FOR YOU
Tomatoes are a good source of vitamins A and C. They also contain significant amounts of the antioxidants lycopene and beta-carotene.

beefsteak

Big, meaty, deep red slicing tomatoes; rich and tangy

BEST FOR: Salads, slicing, sauce, baking, stuffing

GOOD TO KNOW: Classic slicing tomato with reliably good flavor and texture in season

yellow grape

Small, yellow to orange, firm; sweet and mildly flavored

BEST FOR: Snacking, salads

GOOD TO KNOW: Very attractive when mixed with other tomato colors

red grape

Small, red, firm; mild flavor

BEST FOR: Snacking, salads

GOOD TO KNOW: Can be bland outside of tomato season

green

Unripe tomatoes, very firm and tart

BEST FOR: Roasting, baking, grilling, pickling

GOOD TO KNOW: Generally considered too tart to eat raw, but excellent for everything from pan-frying to grilling

hydroponic

Medium-sized, bright red; juicy, with mild to deep flavor and tang

BEST FOR: Sauce, roasting, baking, stuffing

GOOD TO KNOW: Also known as vine tomatoes; versatility and fairly reliable flavor make them a good choice outside of tomato season

kumato

Medium-sized, dark brown to green; firm, juicy, and sweet

BEST FOR: Salads, slicing

GOOD TO KNOW: Greenhouse grown variety developed for good flavor and long shelf life; good choice outside of tomato season

heirloom

Variable shapes and flavors and a rainbow of colors

BEST FOR: Salads, slicing, snacks, stuffing

GOOD TO KNOW: Hundreds of unique varieties available from growers large and small; flavors can vary from sweet to tangy to fruity to bland

yellow

Medium to large, bright yellow to orange; very sweet, fruity and juicy with low acid

BEST FOR: Salads, slicing, sauce, roasting, stuffing

GOOD TO KNOW: Most yellow tomatoes are exceptionally sweet; very attractive when mixed with other tomato colors

cherry

Small, red-orange to red; sweet, juicy and aromatic

BEST FOR: Snacking, salads

GOOD TO KNOW: A real treat at their best, but can be bland outside of tomato season; yellow, green, or orange varieties sometimes available

plum

Medium-sized light to bright red; very firm with mild flavor

BEST FOR: Sauce, roasting

GOOD TO KNOW: Also known as Roma; good choice for cooking outside of tomato season, especially when roasted to concentrate flavor

campari

Small, round, remarkably sweet

BEST FOR: Salads, snacking, stuffing and baking

GOOD TO KNOW: A good option year-round if you can find them

WINTER SQUASH

No other vegetable ushers in the cooler months like winter squash. From burnt-orange pumpkins ripening on the vine to the colorful, oddly shaped varieties found on market stands, the arrival of these festive vegetables each fall is a welcome sign of the change of seasons. All varieties belong to the genus Cucurbita, distinguished by their hard shells, golden to orange flesh, and long shelf lives.

IN SEASON
October to January

⇥ CHOOSING & STORING

• Look for squash that have hard, unblemished skin. Unless the skin itself is green, it should not contain any pale or dark green spots, an indication of immaturity.
• The shell should be neither shiny nor dull. It should have a matte finish.
• Stems should be firm, dry, and sturdy, not skinny and limp. Avoid purchasing pumpkins without stems.
• When purchasing squash that has been cut up, look for slightly moist, tight-grained flesh.
• If stored in a cool, dry area, whole squash will keep for months. Or store on the counter 1 to 2 weeks. (They'll look lovely there, too.) There is no need to refrigerate whole squash.

⇥ USE 'EM UP!

• Because of their extremely hard shells, cutting large winter squash requires special care. Select a heavy knife or cleaver. A rubber mallet is also a helpful tool. Place the squash on a towel to prevent it from sliding around, and cut off the ends. Insert the tip of the knife into the squash and work it down the side, using the mallet to hit the knife into the squash until it splits.
• Alternatively, bake the squash whole until it is just softened; cut it open, remove the seeds, and continue baking until cooked through. Be sure to pierce a whole squash in a number of places before baking to prevent it from bursting open.
• Squash seeds may be roasted and served as a snack or garnish for soups or salads. Rinse seeds to remove flesh, pat dry, and spread in a single layer on a parchment-lined baking sheet. Bake in a 325°F oven until lightly toasted, about 15 minutes.
• Stuff smaller squash, such as acorn or miniature pumpkins, and serve in its own shell.
• As an alternative to pasta, serve cooked strands of spaghetti squash with marinara sauce.
• Pair squash with sage, rosemary, garlic, chili, cumin, ginger, nutmeg, curry, ginger, clove, lime, onions, garlic, apples, and cheeses.

⇥ GOOD FOR YOU

Winter squash is an excellent source of vitamins A and C as well as potassium and dietary fiber.

acorn

Small, with ridged green or green and orange exterior and sweet, dense, slightly fibrous flesh

BEST FOR: Baking, roasting, steaming

GOOD TO KNOW: A very hard, deeply ridged shell makes it difficult to peel when raw; peel after cooking if your recipe requires it

pumpkin

Small to very large, with ridged, thick skin; sweet and creamy or bland and watery depending on variety

BEST FOR: Purees

GOOD TO KNOW: Avoid disappointment by cooking only with "pie pumpkins." Sugar Baby and Sweetie Pie are two common varieties with good flavor and firmer texture

calabaza

Medium to large, with mottled green to orange skin and lightly sweet, fresh-tasting flesh that can be watery

BEST FOR: Roasting, purees, soups

GOOD TO KNOW: Also known as West Indian pumpkin; grown in warm climates, so available year-round

kabocha

Small to medium, with blue-green to orange skin; very smooth, deeply flavored, honey-sweet

BEST FOR: Baking, roasting, steaming, purees, soups

GOOD TO KNOW: Sometimes called Japanese pumpkin

spaghetti

Buttery yellow squash with very mild, lightly sweet flesh that separates into long strands after cooking

BEST FOR: Roasting, steaming

GOOD TO KNOW: Excellent topped with sauce, soaking up gravy, or tossed with herbs and olive oil or butter

delicata squash

Small and oblong with festive stripes; creamy, very sweet, dense flesh with a caramel-like flavor

BEST FOR: Baking, steaming, purees

GOOD TO KNOW: One of the tastiest small, single-serving squashes available

miniature pumpkin

Tiny, slightly flattened orange to cream-colored and deeply ridged; nutty, sweet, tender

BEST FOR: Baking, steaming

GOOD TO KNOW: One of the smallest winter squashes, ideal for individual servings

butternut

Medium-sized, smooth, buff-colored and bell-shaped, with very smooth, buttery, sweet, nutty flesh

BEST FOR: Baking, roasting, steaming, purees, soups

GOOD TO KNOW: Smooth skin and abundant flesh make it ideal for peeling and cutting into chunks for steaming, boiling, and roasting; top choice for making soups and purees

carnival

Very colorful, striped to speckled skin with deep ridges; sweet, rich, dense flesh

BEST FOR: Baking, steaming

GOOD TO KNOW: A cross between an acorn squash and a dumpling squash; flamboyantly colored skin and good flavor make it ideal for halving and baking

sweet dumpling

Very small with ridged skin; sweet, rich flesh

BEST FOR: Baking, steaming

GOOD TO KNOW: One of the smallest winter squashes, ideal for individual servings

turban

Medium to large, with a round base and brilliantly colored "hat" on top; nutty, lightly sweet flesh

BEST FOR: Roasting, steaming

GOOD TO KNOW: A popular harvest ornament, but also edible

hubbard

Medium to very large, with thick blue-gray to green or orange skin; sweet, smooth flesh

BEST FOR: Baking, roasting, stewing, purees, soups

GOOD TO KNOW: Hubbards are extremely decorative but may have skin so tough that cutting into them becomes difficult

ZUCCHINI & YELLOW SQUASH

Zucchini originated in the New World, and together with corn and beans served as a basis for the cuisines of North American and South American Indians. Unlike their winter squash cousins, zucchini and yellow squash (sometimes called summer squash) are eaten when they are young and tender and have not yet developed fully mature seeds.

⇢ CHOOSING & STORING

• Bigger is not better. Small or medium-size zucchini and yellow squash are the most flavorful. Look for squash that are 5 to 6 inches long and about 1 to 2 inches in diameter (a little wider for the widest part of yellow squash) with close to 1 inch of stem still attached.
• An average zucchini, about 6 inches long, weighs between 4 and 6 ounces. One pound of squash yields approximately 4 cups grated or 3½ cups diced or sliced.
• The skin on zucchini and yellow squash should be smooth, somewhat shiny, and unblemished.
• Store summer squash in a perforated plastic bag in the crisper drawer of the refrigerator 4 to 5 days.
• Other varieties of summer squash closely related to zucchini and interchangeable in most dishes include yellow squash; green-and-white striped Neapolitan squash; flying saucer–shaped patty pan squash; and yellow crookneck or gooseneck squash, named for its slender, curved neck.

⇢ USE 'EM UP!

• The versatility of zucchini and yellow squash is almost limitless. It's delicious grilled, baked, and broiled. Add it to stir-fries, soups, pastas, breads (sweet and savory), and even desserts. Cut it into ribbons to resemble pasta and serve it cooked or raw. It makes a perfect container for your favorite stuffing, and even lends itself to being pickled.
• Because there's no need to peel or seed young zucchini, it's perfect for eating raw and in salads.
• To boost nutrition, add grated zucchini to your favorite dishes, such as macaroni and cheese, lasagna, and meat loaf.
• Finely textured, delicately flavored zucchini flowers can be used in numerous ways. Add them to cooked vegetable dishes, soups, and sautés; fold them into omelets, risottos, and pastas; or simply toss with summer greens and herbs for a refreshing salad. They're also delicious and beautiful when stuffed with ground meat, soft cheeses, or cooked grains.

⇢ GOOD FOR YOU

One cup of cooked zucchini provides more than 30 percent of the recommended daily intake of vitamin C plus a dose of vitamin A and potassium.

OUR FRESHEST RECIPES

Welcome to more than 125 easy, delicious ways to make the most of your produce. We start with fruits, taking you from apples to watermelon with new and classic dishes for these naturally sweet treats. Then we move on to the realm of vegetables, bringing you superb recipes for everyone's favorites, from artichokes to zucchini.

FRUITS

Get ready to explore the wonderful world of fruits in recipes both sweet and savory. Our delicious, innovative dishes give you options for every meal of the day, from breakfast to dinner, with some tasty stops for snacks (and dessert!) along the way.

pg. 88

pg. 106

pg. 117

Wheat Berry Breakfast Salad with Apple

SERVES 4
VEGETARIAN

1 cup wheat berries

½ teaspoon salt

1 apple, cored and diced

1 small pear, cored and diced

1 small seedless orange, peeled and diced

1 kiwifruit, peeled and diced

½ cup seedless grapes, halved

½ teaspoon finely grated orange zest

1 tablespoon lemon juice

1 tablespoon chopped fresh mint

4 tablespoons sliced toasted almonds

1 Bring medium saucepan filled two-thirds with water to boil over medium-high heat; stir in wheat berries and salt. Reduce heat and simmer, covered, until berries are tender but still chewy, 45 minutes–1 hour. Drain in colander and rinse under cold running water; drain again.

2 Combine wheat berries, apple, pear, orange, kiwifruit, grapes, orange zest, lemon juice, and mint in medium bowl. Serve, or cover and refrigerate up to 2 hours. Sprinkle each serving with 1 tablespoon almonds.

Per serving (1 cup salad and 1 tablespoon almonds): 274 Cal, 4 g Total Fat, 0 g Sat Fat, 292 mg Sod, 56 g Total Carb, 15 g Sugar, 10 g Fib, 8 g Prot.

cook's tip

This salad is a fresh, healthful breakfast option to start your day. Add ½ cup plain fat-free Greek yogurt for protein and increase the SmartPoints by 1 per serving.

Curried Red Lentil Soup with Apple

SERVES 4
GLUTEN FREE
VEGETARIAN

2 Granny Smith or other tart apples

1 tablespoon canola oil

2 carrots, chopped

1 sweet onion, such as Vidalia, chopped

3 garlic cloves, minced

1 tablespoon curry powder

5 cups vegetable broth

1 cup red lentils, picked over and rinsed

4 tablespoons plain fat-free Greek yogurt

1 Peel, halve, core, and chop one apple. Heat oil in large saucepan over medium-high heat. Add chopped apple, carrots, onion, and garlic; cook, stirring, until onion is softened, about 5 minutes. Add curry powder and cook, stirring constantly, until fragrant, about 30 seconds.

2 Add broth and lentils to apple mixture; bring to boil. Reduce heat and simmer, covered, until lentils are very tender, about 30 minutes. Let cool about 5 minutes.

3 Puree soup in batches in blender. Return soup to saucepan. Reheat over medium heat.

4 Halve, core, and finely dice remaining apple. Divide soup among 4 bowls. Top evenly with diced apple and yogurt.

Per serving (1½ cups soup, ¼ apple, and 1 tablespoon yogurt): 289 Cal, 5 g Total Fat, 0 g Sat Fat, 1,207 mg Sod, 50 g Total Carb, 14 g Sugar, 18 g Fib, 15 g Prot.

cook's tip

Use caution when blending hot liquids: The heat can cause air in the blender to expand, sometimes enough to blow the lid off. Fill the container only half full and hold the lid down with a towel.

Apple-Jicama Slaw

SERVES 6
GLUTEN FREE
VEGETARIAN
20 MINUTES OR LESS
NO COOK

1½ tablespoons honey

1½ tablespoons cider vinegar

1 teaspoon walnut oil

½ teaspoon salt

⅛ teaspoon black pepper

2 cups lightly packed
shredded Savoy or
Napa cabbage

2 cups matchstick
strips jicama

2 Granny Smith apples,
cored and shredded

2 shallots, finely chopped

½ cup dried cranberries,
chopped

¼ cup chopped walnuts

Whisk together honey, vinegar, oil, salt, and pepper in large serving bowl until blended. Add cabbage, jicama, apples, shallots, cranberries, and walnuts and toss until coated evenly.

Per serving (about 1 cup): 141 Cal, 4 g Total Fat, 0 g Sat Fat, 204 mg Sod, 27 g Total Carb, 17 g Sugar, 5 g Fib, 2 g Prot.

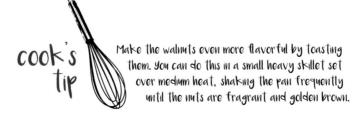

cook's tip

Make the walnuts even more flavorful by toasting them. You can do this in a small heavy skillet set over medium heat, shaking the pan frequently until the nuts are fragrant and golden brown.

Apple-Jicama Slaw

Spiced Apple–Cherry Phyllo Tart

Spiced Apple-Cherry Phyllo Tart

SERVES 8
VEGETARIAN

⅓ cup dried tart cherries, chopped

¼ cup orange juice

3 small Granny Smith apples, peeled, halved, cored, and thinly sliced

3 tablespoons dark brown sugar

¼ teaspoon ground cinnamon

⅛ teaspoon ground cardamom

⅛ teaspoon ground ginger

8 (12 x 17-inch) sheets frozen phyllo dough, thawed

4 teaspoons granulated sugar

---

1 Preheat oven to 400°F. Line baking sheet with parchment paper. Set aside.

2 To make filling, combine cherries and orange juice in small microwavable bowl. Microwave on High until cherries are softened, about 2 minutes. Transfer to medium bowl; add apples, brown sugar, cinnamon, cardamom, and ginger, stirring until combined.

3 To make crust, place 1 sheet phyllo on prepared baking sheet; spray with nonstick spray and sprinkle with ½ teaspoon granulated sugar. Repeat with remaining 7 sheets phyllo and remaining 3½ teaspoons sugar, forming total of 8 layers.

4 Spread filling over middle of crust, leaving border. Lift up phyllo edges and fold over to form 1-inch border (use damp fingers to seal corners so they stay in place). Bake until apples are softened and phyllo is crisp and lightly browned, about 30 minutes. Cool slightly and cut into 8 equal pieces.

Per serving (1 piece): 135 Cal, 2 g Total Fat, 0 g Sat Fat, 96 mg Sod, 30 g Total Carb, 18 g Sugar, 2 g Fib, 2 g Prot.

 **BANANAS**

Steel-Cut Oatmeal with Banana and Walnuts

SERVES 4
GLUTEN FREE
VEGETARIAN

4 cups water
¼ teaspoon salt
1 cup steel-cut oats
2 ripe bananas, mashed
1 tablespoon brown sugar
2 teaspoons unsalted butter
½ teaspoon vanilla extract
¼ cup low-fat (1%) milk
8 teaspoons chopped walnuts

1 Bring water and salt to boil in medium saucepan; stir in oats and return to boil. Reduce heat to low and simmer, stirring occasionally, until oats are tender and water is absorbed, about 25 minutes; remove from heat.

2 Gently stir bananas, brown sugar, butter, and vanilla into oatmeal; stir in milk. Spoon oatmeal evenly into 4 bowls; top each serving with 2 teaspoons walnuts.

 Per serving (about 1 cup oatmeal and 2 teaspoons walnuts): 269 Cal, 8 g Total Fat, 2 g Sat Fat, 161 mg Sod, 44 g Total Carb, 11 g Sugar, 6 g Fib, 7 g Prot

Banana-Coconut Raita

SERVES 6
GLUTEN FREE
VEGETARIAN
20 MINUTES OR LESS
NO COOK

1 cup plain fat-free Greek yogurt

1 banana, finely diced

3 tablespoons unsweetened grated dried coconut

3 tablespoons chopped fresh mint or cilantro

Pinch Indian chile powder or cayenne, or to taste

Stir together all ingredients in small bowl. Serve, or cover and refrigerate up to 1 day.

Per serving (¼ cup): 53 Cal, 1 g Total Fat, 1 g Sat Fat, 17 mg Sod, 7 g Total Carb, 4 g Sugar, 1 g Fib, 4 g Prot.

cook's tip

Raita is a classic accompaniment to spicy dishes like curries and grilled foods such as kebabs or chops. But you can dollop this delicious version on just about anything.

Banana–Chocolate Chip "Ice Cream"

Banana-Chocolate Chip "Ice Cream"

SERVES 4
GLUTEN FREE
VEGETARIAN
NO COOK

4 large ripe bananas

½ teaspoon vanilla extract

¼ cup semisweet mini-chocolate chips

2 tablespoons sliced almonds, toasted

1 Peel bananas; cut into 1-inch chunks and place in zip-close plastic freezer bag. Seal and freeze until frozen solid, at least 2 to 3 hours.

2 Place bananas in food processor; puree, scraping down sides with rubber spatula. Add vanilla and pulse to combine. Transfer to bowl and stir in chocolate chips. Sprinkle each serving with 1½ teaspoons toasted almonds. Serve immediately, or for firmer texture or to make ahead, transfer blended mixture into container and freeze until ready to serve; allow to soften for about 10 minutes at room temperature.

Per serving (½ cup "ice cream" and 1½ teaspoons almonds): 191 Cal, 5 g Total Fat, 2 g Sat Fat, 2 mg Sod, 39 g Total Carb, 21 g Sugar, 5 g Fib, 3 g Prot.

cook's tip

Frozen banana pieces will process into a delicious silky mixture with the consistency of soft-serve ice cream.

BLACKBERRIES

Blackberry-Hoisin Sauce over Chicken

SERVES 4

4 (¼-pound) thin-sliced
skinless boneless
chicken cutlets

½ teaspoon salt

¼ teaspoon black pepper

2 teaspoons olive oil

1 garlic clove, minced

1 teaspoon grated peeled
fresh ginger

⅛ teaspoon red pepper flakes

1 (6-ounce) container fresh
blackberries (about 1¼ cups)

3 tablespoons hoisin sauce

½ teaspoon sugar

2 tablespoons water

2 scallions, sliced diagonally

1 teaspoon toasted
sesame seeds

1 Sprinkle chicken with salt and pepper. Heat 1 teaspoon oil in large skillet over medium-high heat. Add chicken and cook until browned and cooked through, about 3 minutes on each side. Transfer to platter; cover and keep warm.

2 Heat remaining 1 teaspoon oil in same skillet over medium heat. Add garlic, ginger, and pepper flakes and cook, stirring, 1 minute. Add blackberries, hoisin sauce, sugar, and water; bring to boil. Cook, mashing blackberries with back of rubber spatula, until sauce is thick and somewhat smooth, about 5 minutes.

3 Top chicken with sauce and sprinkle with scallions and sesame seeds.

Per serving (1 chicken breast and 3 tablespoons sauce): 203 Cal, 6 g Total Fat, 1 g Sat Fat, 614 mg Sod, 11 g Total Carb, 6 g Sugar, 3 g Fib, 25 g Prot.

Blackberry-Almond Cheesecake Tarts

SERVES 15
VEGETARIAN

15 prebaked mini-phyllo
shells

½ (8-ounce) package light
cream cheese (Neufchâtel)

1 tablespoon granulated sugar

3 tablespoons vanilla
fat-free yogurt

¾ teaspoon grated lemon zest

15 fresh blackberries

1½ tablespoons toasted
sliced almonds

1 teaspoon confectioners'
sugar

 Preheat oven to 350°F. Place phyllo shells on a baking sheet and toast 5 minutes. Let shells cool while you make filling.

2 Using electric mixer on medium speed, beat cream cheese in small bowl until smooth. Beat in granulated sugar, yogurt, and lemon zest until combined. Spoon evenly into phyllo shells; top each with 1 blackberry and some almonds. Dust lightly with confectioners' sugar and serve.

2 SmartPoints value™

Per serving (1 tart): 44 Cal, 2 g Total Fat, 1 g Sat Fat, 39 mg Sod, 5 g Total Carb, 2 g Sugar, 1 g Fib, 1 g Prot.

cook's tip

The filling can be made up to several hours ahead and refrigerated. Let sit at room temperature about 30 minutes before spooning into phyllo shells.

Blueberry Baked French Toast

SERVES 6
VEGETARIAN

2 cups fresh blueberries

6 slices reduced-calorie whole-grain bread, halved diagonally

4 large eggs

2 large egg whites

1 cup fat-free half-and-half

2 tablespoons brown sugar

1 teaspoon vanilla extract

¾ teaspoon cinnamon

¼ teaspoon ground nutmeg

1½ teaspoons granulated sugar

2 tablespoons maple syrup

1 Spray 11 x 7-inch baking dish or 1½-quart casserole with nonstick spray. Scatter 1 cup blueberries in bottom; layer bread halves on top, overlapping pieces as necessary. Sprinkle remaining 1 cup blueberries on top of bread

2 Whisk together eggs, egg whites, half-and-half, brown sugar, vanilla, cinnamon, and nutmeg in medium bowl. Pour egg mixture over bread, covering bread and pressing down slices to coat. Cover and refrigerate at least 1 hour or up to 1 day.

3 Preheat oven to 350°F. Uncover baking dish and sprinkle toast with granulated sugar. Bake, uncovered, until puffed and lightly browned, about 30 minutes. Cool 5 minutes before serving. Drizzle each serving with 1 teaspoon maple syrup.

Per serving (2 toast halves and 1 teaspoon syrup): 188 Cal, 5 g Total Fat, 2 g Sat Fat, 195 mg Sod, 29 g Total Carb, 16 g Sugar, 4 g Fib, 10 g Prot.

Blueberry-Peach Gelatin Terrine

SERVES 8
GLUTEN FREE

½ cup lemon juice

2 (¼-ounce) envelopes
unflavored gelatin

½ cup sugar

1½ cups water

Pinch salt

2 (6-ounce) containers
blueberries

3 small peaches, halved,
pitted, and chopped, or
2 cups chopped unsweetened
frozen sliced peaches

1 teaspoon finely grated
lemon zest

Fresh mint leaves for garnish

1 Place lemon juice in cup. Sprinkle gelatin over top. Set aside 5 minutes.

2 Heat sugar, water, and salt in medium saucepan over high heat, stirring occasionally, until mixture boils and sugar is dissolved, about 5 minutes. Remove saucepan from heat; stir in lemon juice and gelatin mixture. Return to heat and stir until gelatin melts, about 5 minutes. Pour mixture through sieve set over medium bowl.

3 Combine blueberries, peaches, and zest in 4½ x 8½-inch loaf pan. Pour gelatin mixture over fruit, pressing on fruit so that it is submerged. Cover with plastic wrap and refrigerate until thoroughly chilled and set, at least 4 hours or up to 2 days.

4 To serve, run thin knife around edge of terrine to loosen from pan. Dip bottom of pan into large bowl of hot water for 5 seconds. Unmold terrine by inverting it onto platter, shaking pan gently to help release it. Cut into 8 (1-inch-thick) slices and garnish with mint.

Per serving (1 slice): 119 Cal, 0 g Total Fat, 0 g Sat Fat, 52 mg Sod, 25 g Total Carb, 21 g Sugar, 2 g Fib, 7 g Prot.

Roast Salmon with Warm Blueberry Vinaigrette

SERVES 4
GLUTEN FREE

1 teaspoon unsalted butter

1 large shallot, minced

1 cup fresh or frozen unsweetened thawed blueberries

2 tablespoons balsamic vinegar

1 tablespoon maple syrup

2 tablespoons water

1 teaspoon chopped fresh rosemary

½ teaspoon salt

4 (5-ounce) skinless wild salmon fillets

½ teaspoon cracked black pepper

1 tablespoon chopped chives

1 Preheat oven to 400°F. Line baking sheet with foil and spray with nonstick spray.

2 Heat butter in small saucepan over medium heat; add shallot. Cook, stirring constantly, until softened, 1–2 minutes. Stir in blueberries, vinegar, maple syrup, water, rosemary, and ¼ teaspoon salt. Increase heat to medium-high and cook, stirring occasionally and pressing berries with back of spatula to crush, until mixture is thickened, about 5 minutes.

3 Meanwhile, sprinkle pepper and remaining ¼ teaspoon salt on salmon; place on prepared baking sheet. Bake until salmon is just slightly pink at center, 8–10 minutes. Spoon warm blueberry sauce evenly over salmon and sprinkle with chives.

 Per serving (1 fillet and ¼ cup sauce): 237 Cal, 7 g Total Fat, 2 g Sat Fat, 400 mg Sod, 12 g Total Carb, 8 g Sugar, 1 g Fib, 29 g Prot.

cook's tip

If you prefer, you can grill the salmon rather than bake it: Just spray the fish with nonstick spray and grill over medium heat for about 4 minutes per side.

*Roast Salmon with Warm
Blueberry Vinaigrette*

*Creamy Melon and
Cucumber Salad*

Creamy Melon and Cucumber Salad

SERVES 6
GLUTEN FREE
VEGETARIAN
20 MINUTES OR LESS
NO COOK

1 large ripe cantaloupe or honeydew melon, peeled, seeded, and diced (about 4 cups)

1 English (seedless) cucumber, peeled and chopped (about 2 cups)

4 scallions, thinly sliced

2 tablespoons plain fat-free yogurt

2 tablespoons lemon juice

1 teaspoon salt

2 tablespoons chopped fresh mint

Toss together melon, cucumber, scallions, yogurt, lemon juice, and salt in large bowl. (Can be covered and refrigerated up to 1 day.) Serve sprinkled with mint.

Per serving (about 1 cup): 61 Cal, 0 g Total Fat, 0 g Sat Fat, 416 mg Sod, 15 g Total Carb, 12 g Sugar, 2 g Fib, 2 g Prot.

cook's tip

This refreshing melon salad can be served as a first course or side dish. Top it with shrimp or diced smoked tofu for a terrific light meal.

Honeydew-Basil Sorbet

SERVES 8
GLUTEN FREE
VEGETARIAN

½ cup water

3 tablespoons sugar

30 fresh basil leaves, finely chopped (about ¾ cup)

1 ripe honeydew melon, peeled and seeded

3 tablespoons lime juice

1 Combine water, sugar, and basil in small saucepan. Bring to boil over medium-high heat; boil 1 minute. Reduce heat and simmer 5 minutes; remove from heat and let cool.

2 Meanwhile, cut melon into cubes; transfer to food processor and puree. (You will have about 4 cups pulp.)

3 Mix together cooled basil syrup, melon pulp, and lime juice in medium bowl. Pour into ice-cream maker and freeze according to manufacturer's instructions. Transfer to freezer container and freeze until firm. Let stand about 10 minutes at room temperature for easy serving.

Per serving (about ⅔ cup): 76 Cal, 0 g Total Fat, 0 g Sat Fat, 17 mg Sod, 20 g Total Carb, 15 g Sugar, 1 g Fib, 1 g Prot.

Honeydew-Basil
Sorbet

Cantaloupe and Bocconcini Salad

SERVES 4
GLUTEN FREE
VEGETARIAN
20 MINUTES OR LESS
NO COOK

1 tablespoon lime juice

2 teaspoons extra-virgin
olive oil

2 tablespoons chopped
fresh basil or mint

¼ teaspoon salt

¼ teaspoon black pepper

1 small ripe cantaloupe,
halved and seeded

4 ounces bocconcini (small
fresh mozzarella balls),
halved

3 cups firmly packed
baby arugula

1 To make dressing, whisk together lime juice, oil, basil, salt, and pepper in large serving bowl.

2 With melon baller, scoop cantaloupe into 1-inch balls; add to dressing in bowl. Add bocconcini and arugula; toss until combined.

Per serving (1 cup): 145 Cal, 9 g Total Fat, 4 g Sat Fat, 342 mg Sod, 10 g Total Carb, 9 g Sugar, 1 g Fib, 7 g Prot.

cook's tip

If you like, you can make this salad using honeydew instead of cantaloupe. You will need about 2½ cups honeydew balls.

Fresh Cherry Parfaits

SERVES 4
GLUTEN FREE
VEGETARIAN
NO COOK

1 pound fresh sweet cherries,
pitted and halved
or quartered

1 tablespoon sugar

¼ teaspoon almond extract

⅛ teaspoon salt

1 cup plain fat-free
Greek yogurt

1 tablespoon honey

1 Stir together cherries, sugar, almond extract, and salt in medium bowl; let stand at room temperature until cherries release some juice, about 15 minutes.

2 Mix together yogurt and honey in small bowl. Evenly divide yogurt mixture and cherries to make 4 layers in 4 parfait glasses or small wineglasses.

 Per serving (¾ cup): 121 Cal, 0 g Total Fat, 0 g Sat Fat, 93 mg Sod, 24 g Total Carb, 21 g Sugar, 2 g Fib, 7 g Prot.

cook's tip Toasted almonds make a delicious garnish for these parfaits. Sprinkle 1 tablespoon sliced almonds on top of each and increase the SmartPoints by 1.

Sweet Cherry Bruschetta

SERVES 6
VEGETARIAN
20 MINUTES OR LESS

1½ cups sweet cherries, pitted
and quartered

2 teaspoons sugar

¼ cup (2 ounces) herbed
goat cheese

12 thin (½-inch-thick) slices
multigrain baguette (about
3¾ ounces), toasted

1 tablespoon honey

Freshly ground black pepper
to taste

1 Stir together cherries and sugar in small bowl; let stand 10 minutes.

2 Spread goat cheese evenly on toasted bread. Top evenly with cherries, drizzle with honey, and sprinkle with pepper.

Per serving (2 pieces): 117 Cal, 3 g Total Fat, 2 g Sat Fat, 155 mg Sod, 18 g Total Carb, 9 g Sugar, 1 g Fib, 4 g Prot.

cook's tip

Not only does this tasty recipe help you make the most of cherry season, its combination of sweet and savory flavors makes it a great snack or appetizer, dessert, or even a breakfast.

Sweet Cherry
Bruschetta

 **CLEMENTINES**

Mexican-Style Clementine and Jicama Salsa

SERVES 8
GLUTEN FREE
VEGETARIAN
20 MINUTES OR LESS
NO COOK

12 small clementines, peeled and coarsely chopped

¾ jicama, peeled and finely chopped

½ small red onion, minced

1 jalapeño pepper, seeded and minced

⅓ cup finely chopped fresh cilantro

3 tablespoons lime juice

1 teaspoon olive oil

1 teaspoon honey

½ teaspoon kosher salt

1 Combine clementines, jicama, onion, jalapeño, and cilantro in medium serving bowl.

2 To make dressing, whisk together lime juice, oil, honey, and salt in small bowl. Pour dressing over clementine mixture and toss until coated evenly.

 Per serving (about ½ cup): 88 Cal, 1 g Total Fat, 0 g Sat Fat, 125 mg Sod, 21 g Total Carb, 13 g Sugar, 5 g Fib, 2 g Prot.

Clementines with Cardamom and Pistachios

SERVES 4
GLUTEN FREE
VEGETARIAN

½ cup water

¼ cup sugar

1 (3-inch) cinnamon stick

2 (2½-inch-long) strips lemon zest removed with vegetable peeler

3 green cardamom pods, crushed

4 clementines, peeled and halved crosswise

4 teaspoons finely chopped pistachios

1 Combine water, sugar, cinnamon stick, lemon zest, and cardamom pods in medium saucepan; bring to boil over high heat. Cook, stirring, until sugar is dissolved and syrup is slightly thickened, about 4 minutes. Remove pan from heat.

2 Arrange clementine halves, cut side up, in 8-inch square baking dish. Pour hot syrup over and set aside until room temperature, at least 2 hours or up to 6 hours. Remove and discard cinnamon stick, lemon zest, and cardamom pods.

3 Place 2 clementine halves in each of 4 dessert dishes. Spoon syrup over and sprinkle evenly with pistachios.

Per serving (2 clementine halves with syrup and 1 teaspoon pistachios): 101 Cal, 1 g Total Fat, 0 g Sat Fat, 2 mg Sod, 23 g Total Carb, 20 g Sugar, 2 g Fib, 1 g Prot.

cook's tip
The longer the clementines soak in the spiced syrup, the more flavorful the fruit will become.

Broiled Grapefruit with
Mango-Honey Glaze

 **GRAPEFRUIT**

Broiled Grapefruit with Mango-Honey Glaze

3 tablespoons mango or apricot nectar

2 tablespoons honey

¼ teaspoon ground ginger

2 small pink grapefruit, halved horizontally

1 Stir together mango nectar, honey, and ginger in cup.

2 With small serrated knife or grapefruit knife, cut around grapefruit halves to separate flesh from peel. Cut between each membrane to loosen sections, but leave sections in shells; discard any seeds.

3 Preheat broiler. Place grapefruit halves on broiler rack; drizzle with nectar mixture. Broil grapefruit about 5 inches from heat until glaze begins to caramelize, about 3 minutes.

Per serving (½ grapefruit): 71 Cal, 0 g Total Fat, 0 g Sat Fat, 1 mg Sod, 18 g Total Carb, 17 g Sugar, 1 g Fib, 1 g Prot.

cook's tip Allowing the nectar glaze to caramelize [turn brown] will give your grapefruit deep, rich flavor.

Spiced Citrus Salad

SERVES 8
GLUTEN FREE
VEGETARIAN

3 tablespoons sugar

1 (2-inch) piece fresh ginger, peeled and grated

3 whole cloves

⅛ teaspoon ground allspice

¼ cup water

3 grapefruit, preferably pink, white, and red varieties

3 oranges, preferably navel and blood oranges

1 lemon, preferably a Meyer lemon

1 Combine sugar, ginger, cloves, allspice, and water in small saucepan. Bring to boil over high heat; boil, stirring, 1 minute. Set aside to cool.

2 Working with 1 grapefruit at a time, cut thin slices from top and bottom of fruit. Set on cutting board and cut down along curve of fruit, removing all peel and white pith and cutting all the way to flesh. Hold whole skinless fruit over large bowl and cut between membranes to release each segment, letting segments and any juice drop into bowl. Squeeze center membranes over bowl to release any remaining juice. Pick out any seeds. Repeat until all grapefruit, oranges, and lemon are sectioned.

3 Strain syrup and pour over fruit. Toss well and refrigerate, covered, until chilled, at least 30 minutes and up to 2 days.

Per serving (¾ cup fruit with syrup): 79 Cal, 0 g Total Fat, 0 g Sat Fat, 2 mg Sod, 20 g Total Carb, 17 g Sugar, 3 g Fib, 1 g Prot.

cook's tip

This sweet and refreshing salad works great as an appetizer, a side dish alongside fish or pork, or as a light dessert.

 **GRAPES**

Baked Tilapia with Grapes and Olives

SERVES 4
GLUTEN FREE

1½ cups seedless red grapes, halved

⅛ teaspoon + ¼ teaspoon salt

4 (5-ounce) tilapia fillets

¼ teaspoon black pepper

⅓ cup pitted Kalamata olives, halved

1 teaspoon olive oil

¼ cup chopped fresh parsley

4 lemon wedges

---

1 Preheat oven to 400°F. Spray 9 x 13-inch baking dish with nonstick spray.

2 Spread grapes over bottom of prepared baking dish and sprinkle with ⅛ teaspoon salt. Roast 10 minutes.

3 Remove pan from oven and stir grapes. Sprinkle tilapia with pepper and remaining ¼ teaspoon salt; place in single layer over grapes. Scatter olives over the top and drizzle with oil. Bake until fish is just opaque throughout, about 15 minutes. Sprinkle with parsley and serve with lemon wedges.

 Per serving (1 tilapia fillet with about ⅓ cup grape mixture): 183 Cal, 4 g Total Fat, 1 g Sat Fat, 369 mg Sod, 12 g Total Carb, 9 g Sugar, 1 g Fib, 27 g Prot.

Easy Grape Granita

SERVES 6
GLUTEN FREE
VEGETARIAN
NO COOK

---

3 cups seedless red grapes

---

 1 Spread grapes in small rimmed baking sheet and freeze until hard, at least several hours or up to overnight.

2 Transfer grapes to food processor and process until grainy. Scoop into 6 dessert dishes and serve.

0 SmartPoints value™ **Per serving** (about ½ cup): 52 Cal, 0 g Total Fat, 0 g Sat Fat, 2 mg Sod, 14 g Total Carb, 12 g Sugar, 1 g Fib, 1 g Prot.

cook's tip Granita, a classic Italian dish, is irresistibly refreshing. Serve it as a treat on a hot summer afternoon, as a dessert, or as a palate cleanser between the courses of a special dinner.

 **KIWIFRUIT**

Kiwi, Orange, and Strawberry Salad

SERVES 4
GLUTEN FREE
VEGETARIAN
NO COOK

1 tablespoon orange juice

2 teaspoons honey

2 kiwifruit, peeled and sliced

2 oranges, peeled and sliced into rounds

2 cups strawberries, hulled and sliced

1 cup seedless green grapes, halved

2 tablespoons chopped fresh mint

Whisk together orange juice and honey in large serving bowl. Add kiwifruit, oranges, strawberries, and grapes; toss gently until coated. Refrigerate, covered, until chilled, at least 1 hour or up to 4 hours. Serve sprinkled with mint.

 Per serving (about 1½ cups): 114 Cal, 1 g Total Fat, 0 g Sat Fat, 3 mg Sod, 29 g Total Carb, 22 g Sugar, 5 g Fib, 2 g Prot.

cook's tip For a change of pace, substitute cilantro or basil—or a combination of both—for the mint.

Open-Face Turkey and Kiwi Sandwiches

SERVES 4
UNDER 20 MINUTES
NO COOK

3 tablespoons light cream cheese (Neufchâtel), softened

1 teaspoon honey

½ teaspoon Dijon mustard

4 slices reduced-calorie whole wheat bread, toasted

1 cup loosely packed mixed spring greens

½ pound thinly sliced lean deli turkey breast

4 kiwifruit, peeled and thinly sliced

Few pinches kosher salt

Freshly ground black pepper

Stir together cream cheese, honey, and mustard in small bowl until well blended. Spread cream cheese mixture evenly on one side of toast slices. Layer evenly with greens, turkey, and kiwifruit. Sprinkle with salt and pepper.

Per serving (1 open-face sandwich): 181 Cal, 4 g Total Fat, 1 g Sat Fat, 781 mg Sod, 25 g Total Carb, 11 g Sugar, 5 g Fib, 15 g Prot.

Open-Face Turkey and Kiwi Sandwiches

Fluffy Lemon-Ricotta Pancakes

Fluffy Lemon-Ricotta Pancakes

SERVES 6
VEGETARIAN

1½ cups all-purpose flour

1 teaspoon baking soda

½ teaspoon salt

1 cup low-fat buttermilk

2 large eggs, separated

½ cup part-skim ricotta

2 tablespoons sugar

2 tablespoons grated lemon zest, plus more (optional) for garnish

1 Whisk together flour, baking soda, and salt in small bowl. Stir together buttermilk, egg yolks, ricotta, sugar, and lemon zest in large bowl.

2 With electric mixer on medium speed, beat egg whites in medium bowl until soft peaks form when beaters are lifted. Stir flour mixture into buttermilk mixture until just combined; with rubber spatula, gently fold in egg whites until no white streaks remain.

3 Spray large griddle or skillet with nonstick spray and set over medium heat. Spoon ¼ cup batter onto griddle for each pancake. Cook until bubbles appear and pancakes are lightly browned, 2–3 minutes. Turn pancakes over and cook until lightly browned on bottom. Transfer to plate and cover to keep warm. Repeat with remaining batter, spraying griddle between batches, making total of 12 pancakes. Garnish with more zest, if using.

6 SmartPoints value™

Per serving (2 pancakes): 202 Cal, 4 g Total Fat, 2 g Sat Fat, 494 mg Sod, 32 g Total Carb, 7 g Sugar, 1 g Fib, 9 g Prot.

cook's tip

Serve the pancakes topped with banana or peach slices or a mix of fresh berries for 0 additional SmartPoints.

Tequila-Lime Shrimp

SERVES 6
GLUTEN FREE

⅓ cup lime juice

2 tablespoons tequila

1½ teaspoons minced seeded jalapeño pepper, or to taste

¾ teaspoon sugar

½ teaspoon chipotle chile powder

¼ cup chopped fresh cilantro

1 tablespoon olive oil

1 garlic clove, minced

½ teaspoon salt

1½ pounds jumbo shrimp, peeled and deveined, tails left on if desired

1 Stir together lime juice, tequila, jalapeño, sugar, chile powder, and 2 tablespoons cilantro in small bowl; set aside.

2 Heat oil in large nonstick skillet over medium heat. Add garlic and salt; cook, stirring, until garlic is fragrant, about 30 seconds. Add shrimp and cook, stirring, until opaque in center, about 4 minutes. Transfer shrimp to serving platter; cover to keep warm.

3 Add lime mixture to skillet and increase heat to high. Cook, stirring, until reduced, about 2 minutes. Pour lime mixture over shrimp; sprinkle with remaining 2 tablespoons cilantro.

Per serving (⅙ of shrimp): 160 Cal, 4 g Total Fat, 1 g Sat Fat, 363 mg Sod, 3 g Total Carb, 1 g Sugar, 0 g Fib, 23 g Prot.

cook's tip

Serve the shrimp over hot cooked basmati or jasmine rice: ½ cup cooked white basmati or jasmine rice will increase the SmartPoints value by 3.

Tequila-Lime Shrimp

Mango-Cucumber Gazpacho

SERVES 4
GLUTEN FREE
VEGETARIAN
NO COOK

3 large mangoes, peeled, pitted, and diced

2 cucumbers, peeled, halved, seeded, and diced

1 yellow bell pepper, diced

1½ cups low-fat buttermilk

1 garlic clove, finely chopped

1 tablespoon lime juice

1 teaspoon seasoned rice vinegar

½ teaspoon salt

⅛ teaspoon hot pepper sauce (optional)

1 Set aside ½ cup mango and ½ cup cucumber.

2 Place remaining mangoes, remaining cucumbers, bell pepper, 1 cup buttermilk, and garlic in blender and puree. Add remaining ½ cup buttermilk, lime juice, vinegar, salt, and pepper sauce, if using; pulse until blended.

3 Transfer gazpacho to medium bowl. Stir in reserved mango and cucumber. Cover and refrigerate until well chilled, at least 2 hours or up to 2 days.

Per serving (1½ cups): 261 Cal, 2 g Total Fat, 1 g Sat Fat, 392 mg Sod, 62 g Total Carb, 53 g Sugar, 7 g Fib, 6 g Prot.

cook's tip

This unusual fruit-and-vegetable gazpacho can also be prepared with ripe papaya or a mix of papaya and mango.

Creamy Mango Spread

SERVES 8
GLUTEN FREE
VEGETARIAN

1 very ripe mango, pitted, peeled and diced (about 1½ cups)

½ cup water

½ cup part-skim ricotta

2 teaspoons sugar

⅛ teaspoon cinnamon

1 Combine mango and water in small saucepan and bring to boil. Reduce heat and simmer, stirring often, until mango is very thick and reduced to ½ cup, about 15 minutes. Cool.

2 Combine cooled mango, ricotta, sugar, and cinnamon in food processor and puree. Spoon into serving dish or refrigerate, covered, up to 2 days.

Per serving (2 tablespoons): 46 Cal, 1 g Total Fat, 1 g Sat Fat, 20 mg Sod, 7 g Total Carb, 6 g Sugar, 1 g Fib, 2 g Prot.

cook's tip

Serve this delicious spread on toast or whole-grain crackers or use it as a dip for celery or apple slices.

Citrus-Basil Salad with Mixed Greens and Walnuts

SERVES 4
GLUTEN FREE
VEGETARIAN
20 MINUTES OR LESS
NO COOK

---

2 oranges

1 small grapefruit

5 cups lightly packed mixed baby salad greens

2 carrots, cut into matchstick strips

⅓ cup thinly sliced red onion

¼ cup chopped toasted walnuts

¼ cup thinly sliced fresh basil leaves

1 garlic clove, minced

1 tablespoon raspberry or champagne vinegar

1½ teaspoons olive oil

¼ teaspoon salt

⅛ teaspoon black pepper

1 Cut thin slice off top and bottom of 1 orange. Stand fruit on cutting board and cut down along curve of fruit, removing all peel and white pith. Hold skinless whole fruit over medium bowl and cut along membranes to release each segment, letting segments and juice drop into bowl. Pick out and discard any seeds. Repeat with remaining orange and with grapefruit. Measure out and reserve ⅓ cup juice.

2 Combine citrus fruit, salad greens, carrots, onion, and walnuts in large salad bowl.

3 To make dressing, whisk together basil, garlic, vinegar, oil, salt, pepper, and reserved citrus juice in small bowl; pour over salad and toss to coat.

Per serving (about 2 cups): 155 Cal, 7 g Total Fat, 1 g Sat Fat, 229 mg Sod, 21 g Total Carb, 12 g Sugar, 7 g Fib, 6 g Prot.

cook's tip Top each serving of the salad with crumbled soft goat cheese for some unexpected richness. Two tablespoons crumbled goat cheese per serving will increase the SmartPoints value by 2.

Lentil Salad with Oranges and Olives

SERVES 4
GLUTEN FREE
VEGETARIAN

1 cup French green lentils (lentilles du Puy), picked over and rinsed

1 teaspoon grated orange zest

¼ cup orange juice

1 tablespoon extra-virgin olive oil

1 teaspoon honey

1 teaspoon chopped fresh rosemary

¼ teaspoon salt

¼ teaspoon black pepper

1 (4-ounce) package baby spinach

2 seedless navel oranges, peeled, halved, and diced

1 small red onion, halved and thinly sliced

10 pitted black olives, sliced

1 Combine lentils and enough water to cover by 2 inches in medium saucepan. Bring to boil over high heat. Reduce heat and simmer, covered, until lentils are tender but still hold their shape, about 20 minutes. Drain. Transfer to large serving bowl and let cool to room temperature.

2 To make dressing, whisk together orange zest and juice, oil, honey, rosemary, salt, and pepper in small bowl. Add to lentils and toss to coat. Add spinach, oranges, onion, and olives; toss to combine.

Per serving (1¾ cups): 261 Cal, 5 g Total Fat, 1 g Sat Fat, 254 mg Sod, 42 g Total Carb, 11 g Sugar, 18 g Fib, 14 g Prot.

cook's tip

French green lentils are grown in the volcanic soil of France's Auvergne region. These small lentils are famous for their earthy flavor and sturdy texture, making them ideal for salads.

Orange Salad with Mint and Orange Flower Water

Orange Salad with Mint and Orange Flower Water

SERVES 6
GLUTEN FREE
VEGETARIAN
20 MINUTES OR LESS
NO COOK

3 medium blood oranges, peeled and sliced into thin rounds

3 medium navel oranges, peeled and sliced into thin rounds

¼ teaspoon orange flower water

2 tablespoons confectioners' sugar

¼ teaspoon cinnamon

24 spearmint leaves

1 Remove any seeds from oranges. Arrange orange rounds on large platter, alternating blood orange and naval orange slices; sprinkle with orange flower water. Cover with plastic wrap; refrigerate until ready to serve.

2 When ready to serve, combine sugar and cinnamon in small bowl; place in fine sieve. Tap sugar mixture through sieve over oranges; scatter on spearmint leaves. Serve cold.

Per serving (1 sliced orange): 85 Cal, 0 g Total Fat, 0 g Sat Fat, 0 mg Sod, 21 g Total Carb, 17 g Sugar, 4 g Fib, 2 g Prot.

cook's tip This beautiful light dessert gets distinctive character from orange flower water, a flavoring distilled from orange blossoms and used in Mediterranean cuisines. Look for it in specialty stores.

 **PAPAYA**

Pork Chops with Green Papaya Salsa

SERVES 4
20 MINUTES OR LESS

1 cup finely diced green papaya

2 tablespoons chopped fresh cilantro leaves

2 tablespoons chopped fresh mint

1 small shallot, finely chopped

½ Thai chile pepper, seeded and minced, or to taste

1 tablespoon soy sauce

1 tablespoon lime juice

4 (5-ounce) lean boneless center cut loin pork chops, trimmed

½ teaspoon salt

¼ teaspoon black pepper

1 To make salsa, combine papaya, cilantro, mint, shallot, chile, soy sauce, and lime juice in a small bowl and toss.

2 Spray large ridged grill pan with nonstick spray and set over medium-high heat until very hot. Sprinkle pork with salt and pepper. Place in pan and grill until instant-read thermometer inserted into center of each chop registers 145°F for medium, about 3 minutes per side. Serve pork with salsa.

 Per serving (1 pork chop and ¼ cup salsa): 234 Cal, 8 g Total Fat, 3 g Sat Fat, 981 mg Sod, 8 g Total Carb, 4 g Sugar, 1 g Fib, 29 g Prot.

 **cook's tip** Serve these deliciously savory pork chops with a side of jasmine rice. A ⅓-cup portion of plain cooked rice per person will increase the SmartPoints value by 2.

Peaches with Riesling Sauce

SERVES 4
GLUTEN FREE
VEGETARIAN

1½ tablespoons water

1 tablespoon sugar

½ teaspoon lemon juice

¼ cup medium-bodied Riesling wine

4 large firm-ripe peaches, pitted and cut into thin wedges

1 tablespoon + 1 teaspoon finely chopped crystallized ginger

1 Combine water, sugar, and lemon juice in small saucepan over medium-high heat. Bring to boil and cook until syrupy, about 2 minutes. Remove from heat and stir in wine mixture; return to boil. Reduce heat to low and simmer until wine mixture reduces by half and is syrupy, 4–6 minutes. Remove from heat and let cool.

2 Combine syrup and peaches in serving bowl and let stand at room temperature, stirring occasionally, at least 10 minutes or up to 30 minutes. Sprinkle with ginger.

 Per serving (about 1 cup peaches with syrup and 1 teaspoon ginger): 97 Cal, 0 g Total Fat, 0 g Sat Fat, 1 mg Sod, 21 g Total Carb, 19 g Sugar, 3 g Fib, 2 g Prot.

cook's tip

You can substitute nectarines for peaches in this recipe if you prefer.

Grilled Stone Fruit with Honey Yogurt and Pistachios

SERVES 8
GLUTEN FREE
VEGETARIAN

2 firm-ripe peaches, halved and pitted

2 firm-ripe nectarines, halved and pitted

2 large firm-ripe plums, halved and pitted

2 large firm-ripe apricots, halved and pitted

½ teaspoon ground nutmeg, or to taste

1 cup plain low-fat Greek yogurt

1 tablespoon honey

¼ teaspoon almond extract

⅓ cup chopped pistachios

1 Preheat grill to medium or prepare medium fire. (Or spray ridged grill pan lightly with nonstick spray and set over medium-high heat.)

2 Sprinkle cut sides of peaches, nectarines, plums, and apricots with nutmeg and spray lightly with nonstick spray. Place fruit cut side down on grill and cook, turning once, until lightly charred and softened, about 10 minutes; transfer to serving platter.

3 Meanwhile, combine yogurt, honey, and almond extract in small bowl. Spoon 1 tablespoon yogurt mixture over each fruit half; sprinkle each with about 1 teaspoon pistachios.

Per serving (2 fruit halves and 2 teaspoons pistachios): 104 Cal, 3 g Total Fat, 1 g Sat Fat, 11 mg Sod, 16 g Total Carb, 12 g Sugar, 2 g Fib, 5 g Prot.

*Grilled Stone Fruit
with Honey Yogurt
and Pistachios*

*Blue Cheese and
Pear Salad*

 **PEARS**

Blue Cheese and Pear Salad

SERVES 6
GLUTEN FREE
VEGETARIAN
20 MINUTES OR LESS
NO COOK

½ cup low-fat buttermilk

½ cup crumbled blue cheese

1 garlic clove, minced

¼ teaspoon black pepper

1 head romaine lettuce, torn
into bite-size pieces

2½ cups lightly packed
baby arugula

3 firm-ripe pears, halved,
cored, and thinly sliced

¼ cup chopped
toasted pecans

---

1 To make dressing, stir together buttermilk, blue cheese, garlic, and pepper in small bowl.

2 Toss together romaine, arugula, and pears in large serving bowl; drizzle with dressing and gently toss to coat evenly. Serve sprinkled with pecans.

 Per serving (about 2 cups salad and 2 teaspoons pecans): 149 Cal, 7 g Total Fat, 3 g Sat Fat, 192 mg Sod, 19 g Total Carb, 11 g Sugar, 5 g Fib, 5 g Prot.

cook's tip

Apples can be substituted for the pears if you like. Choose Granny Smiths for sweet-tart flavor or Golden Delicious for a milder honey-sweet note.

Hard-Cider Poached Pears

SERVES 12
GLUTEN FREE
VEGETARIAN

3 (12-ounce) bottles hard (alcoholic) cider

¾ cup packed light brown sugar

3 cinnamon sticks

8 whole cloves

1 (3-inch) strip lemon zest

½ vanilla bean, split

6 small firm-ripe Bosc pears

¾ cup plain low-fat Greek yogurt

6 teaspoons chopped toasted walnuts

Freshly grated nutmeg

1 Combine cider, brown sugar, cinnamon sticks, cloves, lemon zest, and vanilla in large saucepan. Bring to boil over medium-high heat.

2 Meanwhile, peel pears, halve lengthwise, and remove core with melon baller or small spoon. Place pears in cooking liquid. Cover and adjust heat so that liquid just simmers. Simmer until pears are tender when pierced with tip of paring knife, 10–15 minutes. Remove from heat and let pears cool in liquid.

3 Remove pears with slotted spoon. (Pears may be covered and refrigerated for up to 1 week until ready to serve.) Remove and discard lemon zest. Transfer cooking liquid to skillet and bring to simmer over medium heat; adjust heat and simmer until liquid is syrupy and reduced to 1 cup, about 20 minutes. Discard vanilla bean. Let cool.

4 To serve, place each pear half in small bowl and top each with 1 tablespoon yogurt, 1½ teaspoons syrup, ½ teaspoon walnuts, and pinch of nutmeg. Discard any remaining syrup.

Per serving (1 pear half, 1 tablespoon yogurt, 1½ teaspoons syrup, and ½ teaspoon walnuts): 113 Cal, 1 g Total Fat, 0 g Sat Fat, 10 mg Sod, 21 g Total Carb, 14 g Sugar, 4 g Fib, 2 g Prot.

cook's tip

Bosc pears hold their shape better than other varieties when poaching. The riper the pear, the more flavorful and the less time it needs to simmer before becoming very tender.

Grilled Asian Burgers with Sweet Onion and Pineapple

SERVES 4

1 pound ground lean beef (7% fat or less)

2 small scallions, sliced

3 tablespoons teriyaki sauce

1 tablespoon grated peeled fresh ginger

1 large garlic clove, minced

½ Vidalia onion, cut into 4 (¼-inch-thick) rounds

4 (½-inch-thick) rings fresh pineapple

¼ cup coarsely chopped fresh cilantro (optional)

1 Preheat grill to medium or prepare medium fire. (Or spray ridged grill pan lightly with nonstick spray and set over medium-high heat.)

2 Mix together beef, scallions, teriyaki sauce, ginger, and garlic in medium bowl until blended but not overmixed. Shape into 4 (¾-inch-thick) patties; spray on both sides with nonstick spray.

3 Spray onion rounds with nonstick spray. Place patties and onion on grill rack or in grill pan and cook, turning once, until instant-read thermometer inserted into side of burger registers 160°F and onion is lightly charred and tender, about 8 minutes. Spray pineapple on both sides with nonstick spray and grill, turning once, until lightly charred, about 4 minutes.

4 Place burger on each of 4 plates. Top each with 1 pineapple slice and 1 onion slice, separated into rings. Sprinkle evenly with cilantro, if using.

Per serving (1 garnished burger): 212 Cal, 7 g Total Fat, 3 g Sat Fat, 596 mg Sod, 12 g Total Carb, 7 g Sugar, 1 g Fib, 26 g Prot.

cook's tip

Want to serve the burgers in buns? One reduced-calorie hamburger roll per burger will increase the per-serving SmartPoints value by 2.

Ginger-Mint Pineapple Salad

SERVES 6
GLUTEN FREE
VEGETARIAN
20 MINUTES OR LESS
NO COOK

6 cups fresh pineapple chunks

1 tablespoon sugar

1 tablespoon lime juice

2 teaspoons grated lime zest

1 teaspoon grated peeled
fresh ginger

2 tablespoons thinly sliced
fresh mint plus small
leaves for garnish

1 Toss together pineapple, sugar, lime juice and zest, and ginger in large serving bowl; refrigerate, tossing occasionally, until sugar dissolves and mixture is chilled, at least 10 minutes or up to 1 day.

2 Just before serving, toss salad with sliced mint leaves and garnish with whole mint leaves.

1 SmartPoints value

Per serving (1 cup): 92 Cal, 0 g Total Fat, 0 g Sat Fat, 3 mg Sod, 24 g Total Carb, 18 g Sugar, 2 g Fib, 1 g Prot.

cook's tip

This salad makes a refreshingly light dessert, or serve it as a side dish that's a classic accompaniment to ham, pork chops, or Asian dishes.

*Ginger-Mint
Pineapple Salad*

Sugar-Roasted Plums with Balsamic and Rosemary

SERVES 4
GLUTEN FREE
VEGETARIAN

4 red or black plums,
halved and pitted

2 tablespoons
balsamic vinegar

3 tablespoons brown sugar

2 teaspoons minced
fresh rosemary

1 Set rack in center of oven and preheat oven to 400°F. Spray 9-inch square baking dish with nonstick spray.

2 Arrange plums cut side up in baking dish. Drizzle plums with vinegar; sprinkle with brown sugar and rosemary. Roast until juices are bubbling and plums are tender, about 20 minutes.

Per serving (2 plum halves): 62 Cal, 0 g Total Fat, 0 g Sat Fat, 4 mg Sod, 16 g Total Carb, 14 g Sugar, 1 g Fib, 1 g Prot.

cook's tip

These sweet-and-savory plums make a fabulous dessert, or try them as a side dish with grilled meat or poultry.

Plum Dessert Parfaits with Yogurt and Almonds

SERVES 4
GLUTEN FREE
VEGETARIAN

2 firm-ripe plums, pitted and diced

1 tablespoon honey

¼ teaspoon cinnamon

¼ teaspoon finely grated lemon zest

Pinch salt

1½ cups vanilla fat-free Greek yogurt

¼ cup sliced almonds, toasted

1 Toss together plums, honey, and cinnamon in medium nonstick skillet. Set over medium heat and cook, stirring frequently, until plums soften and mixture becomes saucy, about 3 minutes. Spoon into small bowl and stir in lemon zest and salt; refrigerate until chilled, at least 30 minutes or up to 1 day.

2 Spoon 1½ tablespoons plum mixture into each of 4 (6-ounce) custard cups or parfait glasses; top each with 3 tablespoons yogurt. Repeat to make one more layer of each; sprinkle 1 table-spoon almonds over each parfait.

Per serving (1 parfait): 127 Cal, 3 g Total Fat, 0 g Sat Fat, 109 mg Sod, 18 g Total Carb, 15 g Sugar, 2 g Fib, 9 g Prot.

*Flank Steak with
Pomegranate Couscous*

POMEGRANATE

Flank Steak with Pomegranate Couscous

SERVES 4

1 teaspoon ground cumin

½ teaspoon cracked
black pepper

½ teaspoon salt

1 (1-pound) lean flank
steak, trimmed

1 cup chicken broth

¾ cup whole wheat couscous

½ English cucumber, diced

¼ cup chopped fresh
cilantro leaves

1 cup pomegranate seeds

½ teaspoon finely grated
orange zest

2 tablespoons orange juice

2 teaspoons olive oil

1 Spray ridged grill pan lightly with nonstick spray and set over medium-high heat.

2 Combine cumin, pepper, and ¼ teaspoon salt in small bowl; rub on both sides of steak. Cook steak until instant-read thermometer inserted into side of steak registers 145°F for medium, 4–5 minutes per side. Transfer to cutting board and let rest 5 minutes.

3 Meanwhile, combine broth and remaining ¼ teaspoon salt in medium saucepan and bring to boil over high heat. Stir in couscous, remove from heat, cover, and let stand 5 minutes.

4 Fluff couscous with fork and stir in cucumber, cilantro, pomegranate seeds, orange zest, and orange juice. Slice steak into 20 thin slices and serve over couscous, drizzled with oil.

Per serving (5 slices steak and 1¼ cups couscous mixture): 351 Cal, 10 g Total Fat, 3 g Sat Fat, 553 mg Sod, 34 g Total Carb, 8 g Sugar, 6 g Fib, 32 g Prot.

 **RASPBERRIES**

Raspberry-Mustard Vinaigrette

SERVES 8
GLUTEN FREE
VEGETARIAN
20 MINUTES OR LESS
NO COOK

1 cup fresh or thawed frozen unsweetened raspberries

2 tablespoons white-wine vinegar

¼ cup lemon juice

2 tablespoons honey mustard

1½ tablespoons olive oil

1 Press berries through sieve set over small bowl, pressing hard on solids to extract puree; discard seeds.

2 Add vinegar, lemon juice, mustard, and oil to berries, whisking until blended well.

1 SmartPoints value

Per serving (about 2 tablespoons): 40 Cal, 3 g Total Fat, 0 g Sat Fat, 20 mg Sod, 4 g Total Carb, 2 g Sugar, 1 g Fib, 0 g Prot.

cook's tip

If you'd like a more savory dressing, feel free to add salt and freshly ground pepper to taste.

Raspberry-Mustard Vinaigrette

Creamy Raspberry Refrigerator Cakes

SERVES 4
VEGETARIAN
NO COOK

96 fresh raspberries (about 2¼ cups)

1 cup thawed frozen light whipped topping

12 chocolate wafer cookies

1 Line 4 (6-ounce) ramekins with plastic wrap, allowing excess to extend over rims of cups.

2 Fit 8 raspberries in bottoms of prepared ramekins in single layer. Top each with 1 tablespoon whipped topping and 1 cookie. Repeat layering twice; top each cake with final 1 tablespoon whipped topping.

3 Fold plastic wrap over each cake to cover, pressing down lightly. Refrigerate overnight. To serve, unfold plastic from top, invert ramekins to unmold each dessert onto plate.

5 SmartPoints value ™

Per serving (1 dessert): 135 Cal, 4 g Total Fat, 2 g Sat Fat, 140 mg Sod, 23 g Total Carb, 11 g Sugar, 4 g Fib, 2 g Prot.

 **STRAWBERRIES**

Fresh Strawberry Salsa

SERVES 8
GLUTEN FREE
VEGETARIAN
20 MINUTES OR LESS
NO COOK

---

1 (1-pound) container
fresh strawberries

½ cup chopped red onion

½ cup chopped fresh
cilantro or mint

½–1 jalapeño pepper,
seeded and minced

1 teaspoon grated lime zest

2 tablespoons lime juice

½ teaspoon ground cumin

½ teaspoon salt

Hull and finely dice strawberries. Place in medium bowl. Add onion, cilantro, jalapeño, lime zest and juice, cumin, and salt and toss. Use immediately or cover and refrigerate up to 1 day.

Per serving (about ⅓ cup): 24 Cal, 0 g Total Fat, 0 g Sat Fat, 147 mg Sod, 6 g Total Carb, 3 g Sugar, 1 g Fib, 1 g Prot.

cook's tip

Use this unique fruit salsa as a topping for grilled poultry, pork, or seafood or in fish tacos.

Chicken, Strawberry,
and Goat Cheese Salad

Chicken, Strawberry, and Goat Cheese Salad

SERVES 4
GLUTEN FREE
20 MINUTES OR LESS
NO COOK

---

2 tablespoons minced fresh tarragon

2 tablespoons warm water

1 tablespoon white-wine vinegar

1 tablespoon honey mustard

2 teaspoons honey

¾ teaspoon kosher salt

⅛ teaspoon black pepper

1 tablespoon olive oil

6 cups lightly packed spring greens salad mix

2 cups diced cooked skinless chicken breast

2 cups shredded carrots

12 strawberries, hulled and sliced

⅓ cup crumbled reduced-fat goat cheese

1 scallion, chopped

---

1 To make dressing, whisk together tarragon, water, vinegar, mustard, honey, salt, and pepper in medium bowl. Slowly whisk in oil until blended; set aside.

2 Combine greens, chicken, and carrots in large serving bowl; add dressing and toss to coat. Top with strawberries, goat cheese, and scallion.

Per serving (about 3 cups): 264 Cal, 9 g Total Fat, 3 g Sat Fat, 547 mg Sod, 18 g Total Carb, 10 g Sugar, 6 g Fib, 29 g Prot.

Strawberries with Cream Cheese Dip

**SERVES 6
GLUTEN FREE
VEGETARIAN
20 MINUTES OR LESS
NO COOK**

1 (1-pound) container strawberries, rinsed but not hulled

½ (8-ounce) package light cream cheese (Neufchâtel), softened

⅓ cup confectioners' sugar

½ teaspoon vanilla extract

1 Place strawberries on serving platter; hull and finely chop 1 strawberry and set aside.

2 With electric mixer on medium speed, beat cream cheese, confectioners' sugar, and vanilla in medium bowl until blended. Reduce speed to low and mix in chopped strawberry. Spoon into serving bowl; place alongside strawberries for dipping.

Per serving (3 strawberries and 3 tablespoons dip): 89 Cal, 3 g Total Fat, 2 g Sat Fat, 88 mg Sod, 14 g Total Carb, 11 g Sugar, 2 g Fib, 2 g Prot.

*Strawberries with
Cream Cheese Dip*

Watermelon Salad with Cucumber, Scallion, and Feta

SERVES 4
GLUTEN FREE
VEGETARIAN
20 MINUTES OR LESS
NO COOK

Mix together watermelon, cucumbers, scallions, vinegar, and salt in serving bowl. Let stand about 10 minutes. Sprinkle with feta and serve.

Per serving (generous 1 cup): 93 Cal, 2 g Total Fat, 1 g Sat Fat, 244 mg Sod, 18 g Total Carb, 15 g Sugar, 2 g Fib, 3 g Prot.

1 (2-pound) piece seedless watermelon, rind removed and flesh cut into ¾-inch chunks

2 Persian or Kirby cucumbers, halved and thinly sliced

3 scallions, thinly sliced

3 tablespoons red-wine vinegar

¼ teaspoon salt

¼ cup crumbled reduced-fat feta

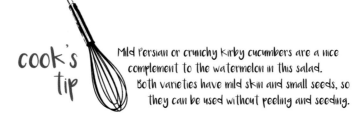

cook's tip

Mild Persian or crunchy Kirby cucumbers are a nice complement to the watermelon in this salad. Both varieties have mild skin and small seeds, so they can be used without peeling and seeding.

Watermelon Pops

SERVES 8
GLUTEN FREE
VEGETARIAN
NO COOK

⅛ large seedless watermelon, sliced, rind discarded, flesh cut into chunks

¼ cup lemon or lime juice

1 tablespoon sugar or honey

 Puree watermelon in batches in blender (you should have approximately 4 cups). Transfer to large bowl and stir in lemon juice and sugar.

2 Pour mixture into 8 (5-ounce) ice-pop molds or paper cups, dividing evenly and leaving ¼-inch space at top. Push wooden popsicle stick into center of each mold or cup. Freeze until hard, at least several hours or overnight. To eat, remove from mold or peel off paper cup.

1 SmartPoints value ™

Per serving (1 pop): 29 Cal, 0 g Total Fat, 0 g Sat Fat, 1 mg Sod, 7 g Total Carb, 6 g Sugar, 0 g Fib, 0 g Prot.

cook's tip

you can substitute ripe cantaloupe or honeydew for the watermelon in this refreshing recipe.

VEGGIES

Reaching your health goals is easier when it's delicious. That's why we delved deep into the vegetable kingdom and rounded up the best and most creative recipes for a rainbow of favorites. From artichokes to zucchini, eating your veggies has never been tastier!

pg. 158

pg. 236

pg. 200

*Herb-and-Garlic
Stuffed Artichokes*

Herb-and-Garlic Stuffed Artichokes

SERVES 6
VEGETARIAN

6 globe artichokes

2 lemons, 1 halved and 1 sliced

2 teaspoons olive oil

1 onion, finely chopped

4 garlic cloves, minced

1 cup plain dried whole wheat bread crumbs

Grated zest of 1 lemon

2 tablespoons chopped fresh thyme

2 tablespoons finely chopped fresh chives

⅛ teaspoon salt

⅛ teaspoon black pepper

2 cups chicken broth

6 tablespoons finely grated pecorino Romano

1 Bring large pot of salted water to boil.

2 Meanwhile, working with 1 artichoke at a time, peel off tough petals around base of artichoke until you get to light-colored petals. Cut off top of artichoke, cutting just below prickly tips of petals. Use kitchen scissors to snip off any prickly tips lower on artichoke. Cut off artichoke stem flush with base; peel stem. Squeeze halved lemon into large bowl of cold water; drop artichoke and stem into water. Repeat with remaining artichokes.

3 Drain artichokes and stems and add with sliced lemon to boiling water; reduce heat to medium. Cook, covered, until knife inserted into bottom of artichoke goes in easily and stems are tender, 30–40 minutes. Using slotted spoon, remove artichokes and stems; drain and let cool.

4 When cool enough to handle, pull out prickly center leaves from artichokes and scrape out fuzzy choke with tip of spoon without cutting into heart. Finely chop stems; reserve.

5 Preheat oven to 375°F.

6 Heat oil in large nonstick skillet over medium heat. Add onion and cook, stirring, until softened, about 5 minutes. Add garlic and cook, stirring, until fragrant, about 30 seconds. Stir in bread crumbs, chopped stems, lemon zest, thyme, chives, salt, pepper, and ½ cup broth. Spoon stuffing into cavities and between leaves of artichokes. Spray with olive oil nonstick spray.

7 Place artichokes in 8 x 12-inch baking dish. Pour remaining 1½ cups broth around artichokes. Cover with foil and bake 20 minutes. Uncover, sprinkle each artichoke with 1 tablespoon pecorino, and bake, uncovered, until cheese melts and stuffing is slightly crisped, about 10 minutes longer. Cool a few minutes before serving.

Per serving (1 stuffed artichoke): 181 Cal, 4 g Total Fat, 1 g Sat Fat, 542 mg Sod, 30 g Total Carb, 3 g Sugar, 10 g Fib, 10 g Prot.

Artichoke Pesto

SERVES 8
GLUTEN FREE
VEGETARIAN
20 MINUTES OR LESS
NO COOK

1¼ cups canned artichoke
hearts (not packed in oil),
drained and rinsed

1¼ cups lightly packed fresh
basil leaves

¼ cup pine nuts, toasted

3 tablespoons grated
Parmesan

3 tablespoons water

1 garlic clove, quartered

½ teaspoon salt

Combine all ingredients in food processor and pulse a few times; then process until finely chopped but not pureed. Spoon pesto into small bowl and press piece of plastic wrap directly onto surface to prevent browning. Serve or refrigerate up to 2 days.

 Per serving (3 tablespoons): 47 Cal, 3 g Total Fat, 1 g Sat Fat, 299 mg Sod, 4 g Total Carb, 1 g Sugar, 2 g Fib, 3 g Prot.

cook's tip

You can toss pesto with hot pasta or use it as a sauce for fish, meats, or grilled veggies. You can even use it in place of mayonnaise on sandwiches.

 **ARUGULA**

Italian-Style Arugula Salad

SERVES 4
GLUTEN FREE
VEGETARIAN
20 MINUTES OR LESS
NO COOK

2 tablespoons red-wine
vinegar

2 tablespoons water

4 teaspoons olive oil

¼ teaspoon salt

¼ teaspoon black pepper

8 cups lightly packed
baby arugula

2 cups thinly sliced cremini
mushrooms

1 cup cherry tomatoes, halved

¼ cup thinly sliced red onion

½ ounce Parmesan shavings
(about 12)

1 To make dressing, whisk together vinegar, water, oil, salt, and pepper in large bowl until blended. Add arugula, mushrooms, tomatoes, and onion; toss until coated evenly.

2 Divide salad evenly among 4 plates and place Parmesan shavings on top.

 Per serving (about 2½ cups): 82 Cal, 6 g Total Fat, 1 g Sat Fat, 216 mg Sod, 5 g Total Carb, 3 g Sugar, 2 g Fib, 4 g Prot.

cook's
tip

For the most authentic flavor, buy imported
Parmigiano-Reggiano instead of domestic Parmesan.
You can make delicious shavings by running a
vegetable peeler over a chunk of the cheese.

Penne and Limas with Arugula Pesto

SERVES 4
VEGETARIAN

4 tablespoons fresh whole wheat bread crumbs (about ½ slice bread)

6 ounces whole wheat penne or gemelli

1 (10-ounce) package frozen baby lima beans, thawed

1½ cups lightly packed baby arugula

1 cup lightly packed fresh basil leaves

2 tablespoons extra-virgin olive oil

2 tablespoons lemon juice

2 tablespoons water

2 garlic cloves, peeled

½ teaspoon salt

¼ teaspoon black pepper

2 tablespoons grated Parmesan

1½ cups grape tomatoes, halved

1 Preheat oven to 350°F.

2 Spread bread crumbs in small shallow baking pan. Bake, stirring once, until lightly toasted, 6–8 minutes. Transfer crumbs to plate and let cool.

3 Meanwhile, cook pasta according to package directions, adding lima beans during last 3 minutes of cooking time. Drain, reserving 1 cup pasta cooking water. Transfer pasta-lima bean mixture to large bowl.

4 To make pesto, combine arugula, basil, oil, lemon juice, water, garlic, salt, and pepper in food processor and puree. Add Parmesan and pulse to combine.

5 Add pesto and tomatoes to pasta mixture, stirring until mixed well. Add reserved cooking water ¼ cup at a time, stirring, until mixture is just moistened. Divide evenly among 4 shallow bowls; sprinkle 1 tablespoon bread crumbs over each serving.

Per serving (1¼ cups): 338 Cal, 9 g Total Fat, 2 g Sat Fat, 355 mg Sod, 54 g Total Carb, 4 g Sugar, 11 g Fib, 15 g Prot.

*Penne and Limas
with Arugula Pesto*

Roasted Asparagus with Pepper Sauce

SERVES 6
GLUTEN FREE
VEGETARIAN

2 pounds regular or jumbo asparagus, trimmed

1 teaspoon olive oil

¼ teaspoon salt

⅛ teaspoon black pepper

1 (7½-ounce) jar roasted red peppers (packed in water)

¼ cup reduced-calorie mayonnaise

1 small garlic clove, peeled

½ teaspoon smoked paprika

1 Preheat oven to 425°F.

2 Put asparagus on nonstick baking sheet; drizzle with oil and toss until coated evenly. Spread asparagus to form single layer and sprinkle with salt and pepper. Roast, shaking pan once or twice, until asparagus are just fork-tender, 10–15 minutes.

3 Meanwhile, drain roasted peppers and pat dry with paper towels. Combine roasted peppers, mayonnaise, garlic, and paprika in food processor or blender and puree.

4 Arrange asparagus on serving plate and serve with pepper sauce on side or drizzle on top.

1 SmartPoints value™

Per serving (⅙ of asparagus and about 2 tablespoons sauce): 83 Cal, 4 g Total Fat, 1 g Sat Fat, 241 mg Sod, 10 g Total Carb, 4 g Sugar, 3 g Fib, 4 g Prot.

cook's tip

The cooking time will depend on the thickness of the asparagus, so be sure to check it a few times during roasting.

Prosciutto-Wrapped Asparagus

SERVES 10
GLUTEN FREE

1 pound regular or jumbo
asparagus, trimmed
(about 20 stalks)

¼ cup light cream cheese
(Neufchâtel), at room
temperature

6 ounces thinly sliced
prosciutto, cut into
20 long strips

1–2 teaspoons balsamic
vinegar, preferably aged

¼ teaspoon black pepper

1 Fill large bowl with ice water. Line large rimmed baking sheet with paper towels.

2 Bring large pot of salted water to boil over high heat. Add asparagus and cook just until bright green and crisp-tender, about 4 minutes. Drain and immediately plunge asparagus into ice water to stop cooking. When cool, spread asparagus on prepared baking sheet and gently roll stalks until dry.

3 Lightly spread dab of cream cheese down center of each strip of prosciutto; place asparagus stalk across end of prosciutto at slight angle. Gently wrap prosciutto around asparagus so it covers stalk, leaving tip exposed. Place asparagus on platter; sprinkle with vinegar and pepper just before serving.

Per serving (2 wrapped asparagus): 85 Cal, 5 g Total Fat, 2 g Sat Fat, 601 mg Sod, 2 g Total Carb, 1 g Sugar, 1 g Fib, 8 g Prot.

Manchego and Avocado Wraps

**SERVES 4
VEGETARIAN
20 MINUTES OR LESS
NO COOK**

2 tablespoons lime juice

2 teaspoons olive oil

1 teaspoon sugar

⅛ teaspoon salt

3–4 drops hot pepper sauce

1 cup lightly packed shredded
green cabbage

1 cup lightly packed shredded
red cabbage

½ cup lightly packed
shredded carrot

¼ cup diced red onion

½ cup chopped fresh cilantro

4 (8-inch) fat-free whole
wheat tortillas

1 Hass avocado, pitted,
peeled, and cut
into ½-inch dice

1 tomato, diced

½ cup shredded
manchego cheese

1 Whisk together lime juice, oil, sugar, salt, and pepper sauce in large bowl. Add green cabbage, red cabbage, carrot, onion, and cilantro; toss until coated evenly. Let stand 10 minutes.

2 Lay tortillas on work surface. Divide cabbage mixture evenly among tortillas. Top each with one-fourth of avocado, one-fourth of tomato, and 2 tablespoons manchego. Roll up tortillas to enclose filling; cut each wrap in half.

 8 SmartPoints value

Per serving (1 wrap): 284 Cal, 14 g Total Fat, 4 g Sat Fat, 446 mg Sod, 34 g Total Carb, 7 g Sugar, 6 g Fib, 9 g Prot.

cook's tip

Manchego is a sweet, nutty, sheep's milk cheese from Spain. It has a dense texture and rich flavor, so a little goes a long way. You can also substitute other firm, flavorful cheeses like Gruyère.

Manchego and
Avocado Wraps

Avocado-Bean Guacamole

SERVES 6
GLUTEN FREE
VEGETARIAN
20 MINUTES OR LESS
NO COOK

½ cup finely chopped red onion

3 tablespoons lime juice

1 (15-ounce) can small white beans, rinsed and drained

1 Hass avocado, pitted, peeled, and coarsely chopped

1 small plum tomato, diced

2 tablespoons chopped fresh cilantro

1 garlic clove, minced

½ teaspoon salt

½ teaspoon hot pepper sauce

¼ teaspoon ground cumin

1 Mix together onion and lime juice in medium bowl; let stand about 10 minutes.

2 Puree beans and avocado in food processor. Add tomato, cilantro, garlic, salt, pepper sauce, cumin, and onion mixture; pulse just until combined.

3 Transfer to serving bowl and refrigerate, covered, until ready to serve or up to 2 hours.

Per serving (⅓ cup): 129 Cal, 4 g Total Fat, 1 g Sat Fat, 212 mg Sod, 20 g Total Carb, 1 g Sugar, 5 g Fib, 6 g Prot.

cook's tip

To keep the guacamole from browning, press a piece of plastic wrap directly onto the surface of the dip; this will keep out oxygen, the culprit in browning.

 **BEETS**

Roasted Beet Salad

SERVES 4
GLUTEN FREE
VEGETARIAN

2 pounds medium beets,
roots cut off and stems
trimmed

2 tablespoons red-wine
vinegar

2 teaspoons canola oil

1 teaspoon Dijon mustard

⅛ teaspoon salt

⅛ teaspoon black pepper

1 tablespoon chopped
fresh oregano

1 Preheat oven to 375°F.

2 Wrap beets individually in foil and place on baking sheet. Bake until tender, 40–50 minutes, depending on size. Let beets cool; use your hands or a paper towel to slip off and discard skins. Slice beets and place in medium bowl.

3 To make dressing, whisk together vinegar, oil, mustard, salt, and pepper in small bowl until blended. Pour over beets and toss until coated evenly. Serve sprinkled with oregano.

 Per serving (¾ cup): 119 Cal, 3 g Total Fat, 0 g Sat Fat, 277 mg Sod, 22 g Total Carb, 15 g Sugar, 6 g Fib, 4 g Prot.

cook's tip The amount of time it takes to roast the beets will depend on their size and freshness. The beets are done when the tip of a paring knife slips into them with just a little pressure.

Borscht with Sour Cream

SERVES 4
GLUTEN FREE

¾ pound beets, shredded
(about 2 cups)

3¼ cups beef broth

½ red onion, finely chopped

½ cup shredded red cabbage

½ teaspoon brown sugar

4 tablespoons chopped
fresh dill

2 tablespoons lemon juice

¼ teaspoon salt

⅛ teaspoon black pepper

¼ cup reduced-fat sour cream

1 In large nonreactive saucepan, combine beets, broth, onion, cabbage, and brown sugar. Bring to boil; lower heat and simmer, covered, until cabbage is tender, about 20 minutes. Stir in 2 tablespoons dill and simmer 5 minutes longer.

2 Stir in lemon juice, salt, and pepper. Ladle into bowls to serve warm, or cover and refrigerate until chilled, at least 2 hours or up to 3 days. Serve garnished with sour cream and remaining 2 tablespoons dill.

Per serving (1 cup soup and 1 tablespoon sour cream): 89 Cal, 3 g Total Fat, 2 g Sat Fat, 949 mg Sod, 12 g Total Carb, 7 g Sugar, 3 g Fib, 5 g Prot.

cook's
tip

Beef broth is the classic base for borscht, but if you prefer a vegetarian version, you can use vegetable or mushroom broth instead.

Stuffed Peppers with Quinoa and Chickpeas

SERVES 4
GLUTEN FREE
VEGETARIAN

1 teaspoon olive oil

1 small onion, chopped

1 small garlic clove, minced

1 (14½-ounce) can Italian-style diced tomatoes

1 cup red quinoa, rinsed well

1 cup water

½ teaspoon salt

4 red bell peppers

1 cup canned chickpeas, rinsed and drained

10 pitted Kalamata olives, chopped

1½ tablespoons prepared pesto

⅓ cup crumbled reduced-fat feta

1 Preheat oven to 375°F. Line small baking dish with foil and spray with nonstick spray.

2 Heat oil in medium saucepan over medium heat. Add onion and cook, stirring, until onion softens, about 5 minutes. Add garlic and cook, stirring, until fragrant, about 30 seconds. Stir in tomatoes, quinoa, water, and salt; increase heat to high and bring to boil. Reduce heat to low and simmer, covered, until quinoa is tender, about 15 minutes.

3 Meanwhile, cut off tops of peppers; remove and discard ribs and seeds. Cut very thin slice off bottom of each pepper so they stand securely; place in prepared baking dish.

4 Add chickpeas, olives, and pesto to quinoa mixture, stirring until mixed well. Spoon about 1 cup quinoa mixture into each pepper. Bake 25 minutes. Remove peppers from oven and sprinkle evenly with feta; bake until feta softens, about 5 minutes longer.

Per serving (1 stuffed pepper): 323 Cal, 10 g Total Fat, 2 g Sat Fat, 859 mg Sod, 48 g Total Carb, 6 g Sugar, 9 g Fib, 14 g Prot.

Stir-Fried Chili Mango Chicken with Peppers

SERVES 4

¾ pound skinless boneless chicken breasts, cut into thin strips

2 teaspoons reduced-sodium soy sauce

2 tablespoons dry sherry or dry white wine

2 teaspoons cornstarch

1 teaspoon salt

⅓ cup chicken broth

1 tablespoon Sriracha

1 tablespoon peanut or canola oil

3 quarter-size slices peeled fresh ginger, smashed

2 green bell peppers, thinly sliced

1 red bell pepper, thinly sliced

1 large firm-ripe mango, seeded, peeled, and cut into ½-inch slices

1 Toss together chicken, soy sauce, 1 tablespoon sherry, 1½ teaspoons cornstarch, and ½ teaspoon salt in medium bowl until cornstarch is dissolved; set aside.

2 Stir together broth, Sriracha, remaining 1 tablespoon sherry, and remaining ½ teaspoon cornstarch in small bowl; set aside.

3 Heat wok or 12-inch skillet over high heat until drop of water sizzles in pan. Add oil, swirling to coat pan. Add ginger and stir-fry until fragrant, about 10 seconds. Push ginger to side of wok; add chicken strips and spread to form single layer. Cook undisturbed 1 minute, allowing chicken time to sear. Stir-fry until chicken is no longer pink but not cooked through, about 1 minute. Add green and red bell peppers and remaining ½ teaspoon salt.

4 Stir broth mixture again and add to wok; stir-fry until chicken is just cooked through and peppers are crisp-tender, about 2 minutes. Remove wok from heat, add mango and toss until combined.

Per serving (1¼ cups): 227 Cal, 6 g Total Fat, 1 g Sat Fat, 820 mg Sod, 22 g Total Carb, 16 g Sugar, 2 g Fib, 21 g Prot.

Stir-Fried Chili Mango
Chicken with Peppers

 **BROCCOLI**

Broccoli with Shallots and Lemon

SERVES 4
GLUTEN FREE
VEGETARIAN
20 MINUTES OR LESS

---

5 cups large broccoli florets with stems

2 teaspoons unsalted butter

1 teaspoon olive oil

½ cup chopped shallots

1 tablespoon very thin strips lemon zest

1 tablespoon chopped fresh thyme

1½ teaspoons salt

½ teaspoon black pepper

---

1 Bring 1 inch of water to boil in wok or large deep skillet over high heat. Add broccoli; cover and cook until crisp-tender, about 3 minutes. Drain and transfer to plate; cover to keep warm.

2 Wipe out wok or skillet. Add butter and melt over medium heat. Add oil and shallots and cook, stirring often, until shallots turn golden, about 5 minutes. Return broccoli to wok along with lemon zest, thyme, salt, and pepper; cook, tossing, until broccoli is heated through, about 2 minutes longer.

 Per serving (about 1¼ cups): 82 Cal, 4 g Total Fat, 1 g Sat Fat, 331 mg Sod, 11 g Total Carb, 2 g Sugar, 3 g Fib, 4 g Prot.

Chicken with Broccoli Rabe and White Beans

SERVES 4

1½ tablespoons all-purpose flour

¾ teaspoon kosher salt

¼ teaspoon black pepper

¾ pound skinless boneless chicken breasts, cut into chunks

2 teaspoons olive oil

1 cup reduced-sodium chicken broth

2 large garlic cloves, minced

¼ teaspoon red pepper flakes

½ pound broccoli rabe, coarsely chopped

1 (15-ounce) can cannellini (white kidney) beans, rinsed and drained

1 teaspoon lemon juice

½ teaspoon grated lemon zest

1 Mix together flour, ½ teaspoon salt, and black pepper on sheet of wax paper; add chicken and toss until coated evenly.

2 Heat oil in large heavy nonstick skillet over medium-high heat. Add chicken and cook, turning, until browned and cooked through, about 6 minutes; transfer to plate. Add broth, garlic, and pepper flakes to skillet; bring to boil, scraping up browned bits from bottom of pan. Add broccoli rabe; cook, covered, until almost crisp-tender, about 3 minutes.

3 Add beans to skillet; cook, covered, until broccoli rabe is tender, about 2 minutes longer. Uncover and mash some beans to thicken sauce slightly. Stir in chicken and cook until heated through; sprinkle with lemon juice and zest and remaining ¼ teaspoon salt.

Per serving (about 1 cup): 271 Cal, 5 g Total Fat, 1 g Sat Fat, 529 mg Sod, 27 g Total Carb, 1 g Sugar, 7 g Fib, 29 g Prot.

cook's tip you can use regular broccoli in place of broccoli rabe in this recipe if you like.

Brussels Sprouts, Watercress, and Pear Salad with Parmesan

Brussels Sprouts, Watercress, and Pear Salad with Parmesan

SERVES 4
GLUTEN FREE
VEGETARIAN

4 tablespoons grated
Parmesan

1 teaspoon grated lemon zest

2 tablespoons lemon juice

1 tablespoon olive oil

¼ teaspoon salt

¼ teaspoon black pepper

1 (10-ounce) container
Brussels sprouts, trimmed
and thinly sliced

2 bunches watercress,
trimmed and separated into
small sprigs (about 8 loosely
packed cups)

2 ripe red pears, halved,
cored, and thinly sliced

1 Preheat oven to 400°F. Line large rimmed baking sheet with parchment paper.

2 Drop Parmesan by tablespoons, 2 inches apart, onto prepared baking sheet, making total of 4 mounds. Bake until golden, 6–7 minutes. Let cool on baking sheet on wire rack. With spatula, remove crisps. Can be stored in airtight container up to 1 day.

3 To make dressing, whisk together lemon zest and juice, oil, salt, and pepper in large bowl. Add Brussels sprouts, watercress, and pears; toss until coated. Divide salad evenly among 4 plates; top each salad with Parmesan crisp.

2
SmartPoints
value

Per serving (2 cups salad and 1 crisp): 141 Cal, 5 g Total Fat, 2 g Sat Fat, 271 mg Sod, 21 g Total Carb, 10 g Sugar, 5 g Fib, 6 g Prot.

Sautéed Brussels Sprouts with Basil and Pine Nuts

SERVES 8
GLUTEN FREE
VEGETARIAN
20 MINUTES OR LESS

2 pounds Brussels sprouts, trimmed and outer leaves removed

1 tablespoon unsalted butter

3 shallots, minced

¼ cup chopped fresh basil

2 tablespoons lemon juice

2 teaspoons kosher salt

¼ teaspoon black pepper

3 tablespoons pine nuts, toasted and chopped

1 Shred Brussels sprouts in batches in food processor.

2 Melt butter over medium-high heat in large heavy nonstick skillet. Add shallots and cook, stirring frequently, 1 minute. Add Brussels sprouts and cook, stirring, until just slightly softened, about 5 minutes. Stir in basil, lemon juice, salt, and pepper. Transfer to serving bowl and sprinkle with pine nuts.

 Per serving (about 1 cup): 89 Cal, 3 g Total Fat, 1 g Sat Fat, 512 mg Sod, 13 g Total Carb, 3 g Sugar, 4 g Fib, 5 g Prot.

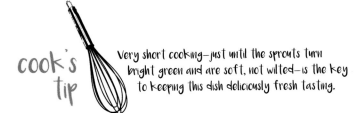

cook's tip

Very short cooking—just until the sprouts turn bright green and are soft, not wilted—is the key to keeping this dish deliciously fresh tasting.

Fillet of Sole with Crispy Ginger and Baby Bok Choy

SERVES 4
20 MINUTES OR LESS

2 tablespoons canola oil

4 (¼-pound) sole fillets

¼ teaspoon salt

2 (2-inch) pieces fresh ginger, peeled and cut into thin matchstick strips

2 tablespoons reduced-sodium soy sauce

2 garlic cloves, thinly sliced

1 teaspoon minced peeled fresh ginger

8 ounces baby bok choy, halved lengthwise

1 Heat 1 tablespoon oil in large heavy nonstick skillet over medium-high heat. Sprinkle fillets with salt and place in skillet. Cook until just opaque throughout, about 2 minutes per side; transfer to plate and cover to keep warm.

2 Add remaining 1 tablespoon oil to skillet. Add matchstick strips of ginger and cook, stirring, about 3 minutes. Add 1 tablespoon soy sauce and cook until all liquid is absorbed. Remove ginger from skillet and set aside.

3 Off heat, coat skillet with nonstick spray; add garlic and minced ginger and cook over medium-high heat 30 seconds. Add bok choy and cook until wilted, about 3 minutes; stir in remaining 1 tablespoon soy sauce.

4 To serve, divide bok choy evenly among 4 plates; top with 1 fillet and one-quarter of reserved ginger strips.

Per serving (1 sole fillet, ½ cup bok choy, and 2 tablespoons crispy ginger): 184 Cal, 8 g Total Fat, 1 g Sat Fat, 527 mg Sod, 4 g Total Carb, 1 g Sugar, 1 g Fib, 23 g Prot.

Braised Red Cabbage with Apples

SERVES 6
GLUTEN FREE
VEGETARIAN

½ small head red cabbage, shredded

2 Granny Smith apples, cut into matchstick strips

2 garlic cloves, minced

2 teaspoons sugar

3 tablespoons red-wine vinegar

½ teaspoon celery seed

½ teaspoon salt

Combine all ingredients in large heavy-bottomed pot. Cook, covered, over low heat, stirring occasionally, until cabbage and apples are very tender, about 45 minutes (add small amount of water if mixture seems dry).

Per serving (about ¾ cup): 45 Cal, 0 g Total Fat, 0 g Sat Fat, 208 mg Sod, 12 g Total Carb, 8 g Sugar, 2 g Fib, 1 g Prot.

cook's tip

The acid in the vinegar helps the cabbage maintain its bright color. Without acid, red cabbage can turn a blue-gray color.

Braised Red Cabbage with Apples

CARROTS

Asian-Style Carrot Slaw

SERVES 6
GLUTEN FREE
VEGETARIAN
20 MINUTES OR LESS
NO COOK

---

2 cups lightly packed shredded or matchstick-cut carrots

2 cups lightly packed shredded red cabbage

1 cup thinly sliced red or daikon radishes

1 cup lightly packed shredded peeled jicama

⅓ cup chopped scallions

3 tablespoons finely chopped fresh mint

2 jalapeño peppers, seeded and minced, or to taste

2 tablespoons sweet orange marmalade or preserves

4 teaspoons rice vinegar

2 teaspoons Asian (dark) sesame oil

½ teaspoon salt

2 tablespoons sesame seeds, toasted

---

1 Toss together carrots, cabbage, radishes, jicama, scallions, mint, and jalapeños in large serving bowl.

2 To make dressing, whisk together marmalade, vinegar, sesame oil, and salt in small bowl; drizzle over slaw and toss until coated evenly. Sprinkle with sesame seeds.

 Per serving (about 1 cup): 85 Cal, 3 g Total Fat, 0 g Sat Fat, 235 mg Sod, 14 g Total Carb, 8 g Sugar, 4 g Fib, 2 g Prot.

cook's tip
This slaw is excellent as a side, but it's also a unique Asian accent to include on burgers or in sandwiches.

Carrot-Ginger Dressing

SERVES 6
VEGETARIAN
20 MINUTES OR LESS

1 cup sliced carrots

½ cup water

2 tablespoons minced peeled fresh ginger

1 tablespoon seasoned rice vinegar

2 teaspoons soy sauce

2 teaspoons Asian (dark) sesame oil

1 teaspoon honey

1 Combine carrots and water in small microwavable bowl; cover and microwave on High until carrots are soft, about 5 minutes.

2 Transfer carrots and water to blender; add ginger, vinegar, soy sauce, sesame oil, and honey. Blend until almost smooth. Scrape into small bowl; refrigerate until slightly chilled, about 30 minutes.

Per serving (about 1¾ tablespoons): 28 Cal, 2 g Total Fat, 0 g Sat Fat, 112 mg Sod, 3 g Total Carb, 2 g Sugar, 1 g Fib, 0 g Prot.

cook's tip

If you like the salad dressing at Japanese restaurants, then try making this healthful version at home. It's excellent drizzled over greens, as a dip for veggies, or as a sauce for seafood.

Creamy Thai Carrot Soup

SERVES 4
GLUTEN FREE

2 cups reduced-sodium
chicken or vegetable broth

1 pound carrots (about 5),
peeled and cut into
1-inch lengths

½ cup chopped onion

1 garlic clove, peeled

2 teaspoons grated peeled
fresh ginger

1½ teaspoons Thai red curry
paste or curry powder

½ teaspoon salt

6 ounces silken tofu, diced

2 tablespoons sliced
fresh mint leaves

1 Combine broth, carrots, onion, garlic, and ginger in medium saucepan; bring to boil over medium-high heat. Reduce heat to low and simmer, covered, until carrots are tender, about 20 minutes. Stir in curry paste and salt; simmer 1 minute to allow flavors to blend. Remove from heat; let cool slightly.

2 Add tofu to soup and puree using immersion blender, or let cool 5 minutes and puree in batches in blender. Return soup to saucepan and cook over medium heat until heated through. Ladle evenly into 4 bowls and sprinkle with mint.

Per serving (about 1 cup): 90 Cal, 2 g Total Fat, 0 g Sat Fat, 613 mg Sod, 16 g Total Carb, 8 g Sugar, 4 g Fib, 3 g Prot.

cook's tip

Tofu adds a tempting creamy texture to this soup without the fat and calories of cream.

 **CAULIFLOWER**

Roasted Cauliflower with Parmesan

SERVES 6
GLUTEN FREE
VEGETARIAN

6 cups cauliflower florets
(about 1 head)

1 tablespoon olive oil

½ teaspoon kosher salt

½ teaspoon black pepper

¼ cup grated Parmesan

1 Preheat oven to 450°F.

2 Toss together cauliflower, oil, salt, and pepper in large bowl. Transfer cauliflower to large rimmed baking sheet and spread to form single layer. Roast, tossing occasionally, until cauliflower is golden brown and crisp-tender, about 15 minutes. Transfer cauliflower to large serving bowl; sprinkle with Parmesan and toss until coated evenly.

 Per serving (about ¾ cup): 63 Cal, 4 g Total Fat, 1 g Sat Fat, 255 mg Sod, 6 g Total Carb, 2 g Sugar, 3 g Fib, 4 g Prot.

 cook's tip

This recipe is extremely versatile. If you like, substitute broccoli, baby carrots, or asparagus for the cauliflower; just keep in mind that roasting times may differ.

Grilled Cauliflower
Steaks with
Homemade Pesto

Grilled Cauliflower Steaks with Homemade Pesto

SERVES 8
GLUTEN FREE

2 cups lightly packed fresh basil leaves

½ cup reduced-sodium chicken broth

¼ cup grated Parmesan

2 tablespoons pine nuts, toasted and cooled

2 garlic cloves, peeled

1 tablespoon olive oil

½ teaspoon salt

1 (1 ½-pound) head cauliflower, cut through stem end into 8 (½-inch-thick) "steaks"

1 Preheat grill to medium or prepare medium fire, or heat ridged grill pan over medium-high heat.

2 Meanwhile, to make pesto, combine basil, broth, Parmesan, pine nuts, garlic, oil, and salt in food processor and puree. Set aside.

3 Lightly spray cauliflower with olive oil nonstick spray. Place cauliflower on grill rack or in grill pan and cook, turning once, until marked and tender, about 10 minutes (if cooking cauliflower on grill pan you may need to work in batches). With wide spatula, transfer cauliflower to serving platter, separating into small sections if you like; spoon pesto over top.

Per serving (1 cauliflower "steak" with 2 tablespoons pesto): 66 Cal, 4 g Total Fat, 1 g Sat Fat, 245 mg Sod, 6 g Total Carb, 2 g Sugar, 3 g Fib, 3 g Prot.

cook's tip

To toast the pine nuts, spread them in a small dry skillet and set over medium heat. Cook, shaking pan occasionally, until the nuts are golden, about 3 minutes. Immediately transfer to a small plate.

Buffalo-Style Stuffed Celery

SERVES 10
GLUTEN FREE
VEGETARIAN
20 MINUTES OR LESS
NO COOK

½ cup light cream cheese (Neufchatel), at room temperature

2 tablespoons blue cheese, softened

½ garlic clove, finely chopped

¼ teaspoon salt

5 large celery stalks, each cut into 4 pieces

2½ teaspoons hot pepper sauce, or to taste

1 tablespoon chopped fresh chives

Stir together cream cheese, blue cheese, garlic, and salt in small bowl until smooth. Spoon rounded teaspoon of mixture into each piece of celery. Drizzle each with about ⅛ teaspoon pepper sauce (or let guests add their own pepper sauce) and sprinkle with chives.

 Per serving (2 pieces): 36 Cal, 2 g Total Fat, 1 g Sat Fat, 195 mg Sod, 2 g Total Carb, 1 g Sugar, 1 g Fib, 2 g Prot.

Lemon-Curry Celery and Chickpea Salad

SERVES 6
GLUTEN FREE
VEGETARIAN
20 MINUTES OR LESS
NO COOK

½ cup plain low-fat yogurt

1 teaspoon finely grated lemon zest

1 tablespoon fresh lemon juice

2 teaspoons honey

1 teaspoon curry powder

½ teaspoon salt

2 cups sliced celery with leaves

1 (15½-ounce) can chickpeas, rinsed and drained

1 large carrot, cut into matchstick strips or shredded

3 scallions, sliced

Whisk yogurt, lemon zest and juice, honey, curry powder, and salt together in large bowl. Stir in celery, chickpeas, carrot, and scallions.

Per serving (1 cup): 98 Cal, 1 g Total Fat, 0 g Sat Fat, 403 mg Sod, 18 g Total Carb, 5 g Sugar, 5 g Fib, 5 g Prot.

cook's tip

Use inner, pale green celery stalks for this recipe: They are more tender and less stringy than the larger outer ones.

Celery Root and Yukon Gold Mash

SERVES 8
GLUTEN FREE
VEGETARIAN

2 tablespoons canola oil

2 onions, chopped

1 pound celery root, trimmed, peeled, and cut into 1-inch chunks

1 pound Yukon Gold potatoes, scrubbed and cut into 1-inch chunks

1 teaspoon salt

½ teaspoon ground white pepper

¼ cup low-fat buttermilk, warmed

2 tablespoons chopped fresh parsley

1 Heat oil in large skillet over medium heat. Add onions and cook, stirring frequently, until soft, about 5 minutes. Cover skillet and continue to cook, stirring occasionally, until onions are golden and meltingly tender, 20–25 minutes longer.

2 Meanwhile, combine celery root and potato chunks in large saucepan and add enough water to cover. Bring to boil over medium-high heat; reduce heat and simmer until tender, about 15 minutes. Drain.

3 Return celery root and potatoes to saucepan and sprinkle with salt and pepper; stir in buttermilk. With masher or wooden spoon, coarsely mash potato mixture; stir in onions and parsley.

Per serving (about ½ cup): 107 Cal, 4 g Total Fat, 0 g Sat Fat, 365 mg Sod, 17 g Total Carb, 3 g Sugar, 3 g Fib, 2 g Prot.

cook's tip

White pepper is usually the seasoning of choice for white mashes and purees like this one, but feel free to use black pepper if you prefer—the difference in flavor is minimal.

Celery Root and Yukon Gold Mash

Slow-Cooker Celery Root and Apple Soup

SERVES 6
GLUTEN FREE
VEGETARIAN

6 cups vegetable broth

2 cups trimmed, peeled, and chopped celery root

3 small apples, peeled, cored, and chopped

1 celery stalk including leaves, chopped

1 large leek, white and light green parts only, thinly sliced and well rinsed

1 small baking potato, peeled and coarsely chopped

1 tablespoon light brown sugar

1 teaspoon salt

¼ teaspoon black pepper

tk teaspoons lemon juice

6 tablespoons reduced-fat sour cream

3 tablespoons chopped fresh parsley leaves

1 Combine broth, celery root, apples, celery, leek, potato, brown sugar, salt, and pepper in 5- or 6-quart slow cooker. Cover and cook 4–6 hours on high or 8–10 hours on low.

2 At end of cooking time, uncover and let cool 5 minutes. Puree soup in batches in blender. Return soup to slow cooker and stir in lemon juice. Cover and cook on high until heated through, about 5 minutes. Ladle evenly into 6 soup bowls. Swirl 1 tablespoon sour cream into each and sprinkle with parsley.

Per serving (1¾ cups soup and 1 tablespoon sour cream): 134 Cal, 2 g Total Fat, 1 g Sat Fat, 1,400 mg Sod, 28 g Total Carb, 13 g Sugar, 4 g Fib, 3 g Prot.

Cranberry-Jalapeño Sauce

SERVES 12
GLUTEN FREE
VEGETARIAN

1 (12-ounce) bag fresh
cranberries

2 jalapeño peppers, seeded
and finely chopped

⅓ cup packed dark
brown sugar

2 tablespoons red wine

Pinch salt

Combine all ingredients in a nonreactive saucepan and bring to boil. Boil 1 minute; then reduce heat to low. Simmer until berries pop and mixture is thick, about 10 minutes. Cool and serve.

Per serving (2 tablespoons): 39 Cal, 0 g Total Fat, 0 g Sat Fat, 27 mg Sod, 10 g Total Carb, 7 g Sugar, 1 g Fib, 0 g Prot.

Corn-and-Barley
Chile Rellenos

Corn-and-Barley Chile Rellenos

SERVES 4
VEGETARIAN

½ cup pearl barley

4 large poblano peppers

1 teaspoon canola oil

1 small onion, chopped

2 garlic cloves, minced

½ teaspoon ground cumin

¾ cup fresh or thawed
frozen corn kernels

½ cup shredded reduced-fat
Cheddar

2 tablespoons chopped
fresh cilantro

½ jalapeño pepper,
seeded and minced

¼ teaspoon salt

4 tablespoons light sour
cream (optional)

Lime wedges

1 Cook barley according to package directions. Drain. Rinse under cold running water; drain again. Transfer to large bowl.

2 Meanwhile, preheat boiler. Line broiler rack with foil; place poblano peppers on foil. Broil 5 inches from heat, turning frequently with tongs, until skins blister, about 10 minutes. Transfer peppers with foil to work surface and wrap in foil. Let steam about 15 minutes.

3 When cool enough to handle, peel blackened skin off peppers. Using sharp knife, make long slit in each pepper; remove seeds and membranes, being careful not to tear peppers.

4 Preheat oven to 375°F. Spray 7 x 11-inch baking dish with nonstick spray.

5 Meanwhile, heat oil in small nonstick skillet over medium heat. Add onion and cook, stirring, until golden, about 8 minutes. Add garlic and cumin; cook, stirring constantly, until fragrant, about 30 seconds. Add onion mixture, corn, Cheddar, cilantro, jalapeño, and salt to barley; stir to combine.

6 Spoon about ¾ cup barley mixture into each poblano pepper, mounding filling and taking care not to tear peppers. Arrange in prepared baking dish. Cover and bake until heated through, 20–25 minutes. Serve with sour cream on top (if using) and lime wedges on side.

Per serving (1 stuffed pepper with 1 tablespoon sour cream): 227 Cal, 5 g Total Fat, 2 g Sat Fat, 252 mg Sod, 40 g Total Carb, 8 g Sugar, 7 g Fib, 10 g Prot.

Collard Wraps with Seasoned Rice

SERVES 4
GLUTEN FREE

2 (¾-pound) bunches
collard greens

1 teaspoon olive oil

1 shallot, finely chopped

1 teaspoon ground cumin

½ teaspoon cinnamon

1½ cups chicken or
vegetable broth

¾ cup brown rice

⅓ cup golden raisins

2 tablespoons chopped
toasted pine nuts

¼ teaspoon grated lemon zest

2 teaspoons fresh lemon juice

¼ teaspoon salt

¼ teaspoon pepper

4 lemon wedges

1 Bring large pot two-thirds full of lightly salted water to boil. Meanwhile, remove thick stems from collard greens, keeping leaf intact. Blanch leaves in boiling water 5 minutes; rinse under cold water and drain. Choose 8 large leaves and place on paper towels to dry. Chop remaining leaves; you should have about 1½ cups chopped. Squeeze excess liquid from leaves.

2 Heat oil in medium saucepan over medium heat. Add shallot; cook, stirring, until just tender, 1–2 minutes. Stir in cumin and cinnamon and cook until fragrant, about 30 seconds. Add broth and bring to boil. Stir in rice. Reduce heat to medium-low and simmer, covered, until liquid is absorbed and rice is tender, about 50 minutes. Fluff rice with fork.

3 Stir together rice, chopped collards, raisins, pine nuts, lemon zest and juice, salt, and pepper in large bowl. Let cool.

4 Place 1 whole collard leaf on cutting board and spoon ½ cup rice filling in center. Roll end of leaf over filling, tuck in sides, and roll tightly like a cigar or burrito. Repeat with remaining leaves and filling. Serve warm or room temperature with lemon wedges.

7 SmartPoints value™

Per serving (2 rolls): 277 Cal, 6 g Total Fat, 1 g Sat Fat, 470 mg Sod, 50 g Total Carb, 9 g Sugar, 8 g Fib, 10 g Prot.

cook's tip

To make the rolls ahead and serve them warm, place collard rolls in a baking dish, cover with aluminum foil, and refrigerate. When ready to serve, reheat rolls in a 275°F oven, covered, 15 minutes.

Collard Wraps with Seasoned Rice

Quick Southern-Style Collards

SERVES 4
GLUTEN FREE

3 slices reduced-fat bacon,
cut into 1½-inch pieces

¾ cup chopped onion

2 garlic cloves, sliced

1 pound collard greens, thick
stems removed and leaves
cut into ½-inch strips
(about 8 cups)

1½ cups water

2 teaspoons cider vinegar

½ teaspoon salt

¼ teaspoon hot pepper sauce,
plus more for serving

1 Cook bacon in large pot over medium heat, stirring occasionally, until it begins to sizzle and releases some fat, 2–3 minutes. Stir in onion. Reduce heat to medium-low and cook, stirring often, until onion is light golden, about 7 minutes. Add garlic; cook, stirring, until fragrant, about 30 seconds.

2 Add collard greens to pot and increase heat to high; cook, stirring, until greens wilt, about 2 minutes. Add water and bring to boil. Reduce heat to low and simmer, covered, stirring occasionally, until greens are tender, about 10 minutes longer. Remove from heat and stir in vinegar, salt, and pepper sauce. Serve with more pepper sauce on side.

Per serving (about ¾ cup): 69 Cal, 2 g Total Fat, 1 g Sat Fat, 410 mg Sod, 9 g Total Carb, 2 g Sugar, 5 g Fib, 5 g Prot.

CORN

Summer Corn, Bacon, and Potato Chowder

SERVES 4
GLUTEN FREE

---

1 medium (6-ounce)
Yukon Gold potato

4 ears sweet corn, husks and
silk removed, kernels cut off

1 small red bell pepper, diced

1 celery stalk, chopped

¼ cup chopped onion

2 cups fat-free milk

4 ounces sliced Canadian
bacon, diced

½ teaspoon salt

¼ teaspoon black pepper

Pinch cayenne

2 scallions, sliced

---

1 With fork, pierce potato in several places; place on plate and microwave on High until tender, about 8 minutes, turning once. Let cool; peel and mash.

2 Meanwhile, spray large saucepan with nonstick spray and set over medium-high heat. Add corn, bell pepper, celery, and onion; cook, stirring, until onion is softened, about 5 minutes. Add milk, bacon, and mashed potato, mixing well. Stir in salt, black pepper, and cayenne. Simmer, covered, 10 minutes (do not let boil). Ladle chowder evenly into 4 bowls and sprinkle with scallions.

 Per serving (1½ cups): 215 Cal, 3 g Total Fat, 1 g Sat Fat, 569 mg Sod, 38 g Total Carb, 13 g Sugar, 5 g Fib, 15 g Prot.

cook's tip

If it's not corn season, you can substitute 2 cups frozen corn kernels for the fresh corn.

Buffalo-Style Grilled
Corn on the Cob

Buffalo-Style Grilled Corn on the Cob

SERVES 8
GLUTEN FREE
VEGETARIAN

¼ cup crumbled blue cheese

2 tablespoons unsalted butter

1 tablespoon minced fresh chives or green part of scallion

2 teaspoons hot pepper sauce, or to taste

½ teaspoon salt

¼ teaspoon celery seed

8 ears sweet corn, husks and silk removed

1 Preheat grill to medium or prepare medium fire.

2 Meanwhile, stir together blue cheese and butter in small microwavable bowl; microwave on High in 7-second increments until butter melts. Stir in chives, pepper sauce, salt, and celery seed until smooth; set aside.

3 Spray corn lightly with nonstick spray. Place corn on grill rack and grill, covered, turning occasionally, until well marked and tender, about 10 minutes. Transfer corn to platter and brush with blue-cheese mixture.

Per serving (1 ear corn): 142 Cal, 6 g Total Fat, 3 g Sat Fat, 238 mg Sod, 22 g Total Carb, 5 g Sugar, 2 g Fib, 4 g Prot.

Creamy Cucumber Dip

SERVES 8
GLUTEN FREE
VEGETARIAN
UNDER 20 MINUTES
NO COOK

---

2 cups plain low-fat yogurt

½ cup reduced-calorie
mayonnaise

1 teaspoon salt

½ teaspoon ground cumin

¼ teaspoon cayenne

1½ cups diced English, Kirby,
or Persian cucumbers

½ cup diced red onion

⅓ cup chopped fresh
mint leaves

⅓ cup chopped fresh dill

In medium bowl, whisk together yogurt, mayonnaise, salt, cumin, and cayenne until combined. Stir in cucumbers, onion, mint, and dill.

 Per serving (½ cup): 97 Cal, 6 g Total Fat, 1 g Sat Fat, 443 mg Sod, 7 g Total Carb, 6 g Sugar, 1 g Fib, 4 g Prot.

cook's tip

Use this refreshing dip as an accompaniment to your favorite raw veggies or as a sandwich spread.

Cucumber-Salmon Sushi Rolls

SERVES 4

1 cup short-grain white rice

1¼ cups water

1½ tablespoons seasoned rice vinegar

2 teaspoons honey

⅛ teaspoon salt

3 tablespoons light cream cheese (Neufchâtel), at room temperature

1 teaspoon wasabi paste

4 (7 x 8-inch) sheets nori

1 (3-ounce) package sliced smoked salmon, cut into strips

1 large carrot, cut into 16 ribbons

1 English (seedless) cucumber, peeled, cut into 16 ribbons

2 tablespoons drained pickled ginger, cut into strips

4 tablespoons reduced-sodium soy sauce for serving

1 Combine rice and water in medium saucepan; bring to boil over high heat. Reduce heat and simmer, covered, until water is absorbed and rice is tender, about 20 minutes. Remove pan from heat and let stand, covered, 10 minutes. Fluff with fork.

2 Meanwhile, whisk together vinegar, honey, and salt in small bowl. Combine cream cheese and wasabi paste in another small bowl. Fluff rice again; stir vinegar mixture into rice until mixed well. Let cool 20 minutes.

3 Place bamboo rolling mat on work surface with slats facing horizontally. Place 1 nori sheet with short side facing you, shiny side down, on mat. Dampen hands with water and spread scant ⅔ cup rice on sheet leaving 1-inch border across top. Spread 2 teaspoons cream cheese mixture crosswise along center of rice. Top with one quarter of salmon, 4 strips carrot, and then 4 strips cucumber.

4 Holding filling in place with your fingers, gently roll mat away from you, using your thumbs to help roll it up, until edges of nori overlap, forming roll. Seal by dabbing water along edge of nori.

5 Transfer roll to cutting board. With sharp knife moistened with water, cut roll into 6 pieces. Repeat with remaining nori, rice, and filling ingredients, making total of 4 rolls. Top evenly with ginger. Serve with soy sauce.

Per serving (6 pieces sushi and 1 tablespoon soy sauce): 261 Cal, 3 g Total Fat, 1 g Sat Fat, 1,110 mg Sod, 47 g Total Carb, 6 g Sugar, 2 g Fib, 10 g Prot.

Mediterranean Eggplant and Olive Stew

SERVES 4
VEGETARIAN

2 teaspoons canola oil

2 onions, sliced

4 garlic cloves, minced

1 cinnamon stick

½ teaspoon ground cumin

¼ teaspoon ground ginger

3½ cups vegetable broth

1 (14½-ounce) can diced
tomatoes

¾ teaspoon salt

¼ teaspoon black pepper

1 large eggplant (about
1½ pounds), cut into
1-inch cubes

½ cup pitted green olives,
coarsely chopped

2 tablespoons golden raisins

1 cup whole wheat couscous

1 Heat oil in large saucepan or small Dutch oven set over medium-high heat. Add onions and garlic; cook, stirring, until onions are softened, about 5 minutes. Add cinnamon stick, cumin, and ginger and cook, stirring, until fragrant, about 30 seconds. Add 2 cups broth, tomatoes, ½ teaspoon salt, and pepper; bring to boil. Add eggplant, olives, and raisins. Reduce heat and simmer, covered, stirring occasionally, until eggplant is tender, about 25 minutes.

2 Meanwhile, combine couscous, remaining 1½ cups broth, and remaining ¼ teaspoon salt in small saucepan; bring to boil over high heat. Remove from heat; cover and let sit until liquid is absorbed and couscous is tender, about 10 minutes.

3 Divide couscous evenly among 4 bowls; ladle eggplant stew evenly on top.

7 SmartPoints value™

Per serving (1½ cups stew and generous ½ cup couscous): 299 Cal, 5 g Total Fat, 0 g Sat Fat, 1,411 mg Sod, 58 g Total Carb, 16 g Sugar, 12 g Fib, 10 g Prot.

Mediterranean Eggplant and Olive Stew

Grilled Baby Eggplant with Yogurt Sauce

SERVES 4
GLUTEN FREE
VEGETARIAN

¾ cup plain fat-free Greek yogurt

2 tablespoons water

¼ teaspoon ground cumin

¼ teaspoon smoked paprika, plus additional for sprinkling

½ small garlic clove, minced

¾ teaspoon kosher salt

3 baby eggplants (1¼ pounds), sliced lengthwise into ½-inch-thick slices

¼ cup thinly sliced fresh mint

---

1 Preheat grill to medium-high or prepare medium-high fire.

2 Meanwhile, to make sauce, stir together yogurt, water, cumin, paprika, garlic, and ¼ teaspoon salt in small bowl. Set aside.

3 Spray eggplant slices on both sides with nonstick spray and sprinkle with remaining ½ teaspoon salt. Place eggplant on grill rack and grill, turning, until lightly charred and tender, about 10 minutes. Arrange on platter and spoon yogurt sauce over; sprinkle with mint and paprika.

Per serving (about 3 slices eggplant and 3 tablespoons sauce): 66 Cal, 1 g Total Fat, 0 g Sat Fat, 382 mg Sod, 10 g Total Carb, 5 g Sugar, 4 g Fib, 6 g Prot.

 **ENDIVE**

Endive-Apple Salad with Sherry Vinaigrette

SERVES 4
GLUTEN FREE
VEGETARIAN
20 MINUTES OR LESS
NO COOK

1 tablespoon sherry vinegar

2 teaspoons olive oil

2 teaspoons Dijon mustard

3 tablespoons warm water

½ teaspoon salt

¼ teaspoon black pepper

2 Belgian endive,
leaves separated

1 red apple, halved, cored,
and cut into thin wedges

3 tablespoons walnuts,
toasted and chopped

4 tablespoons crumbled
reduced fat-feta

Whisk together vinegar, oil, mustard, water, salt, and pepper in large bowl. Add endive, apple, and walnuts and toss to coat. Divide salad evenly among 4 plates. Top each with 1 tablespoon feta.

 Per serving (about 1¼ cups salad and 1 tablespoon feta): 129 Cal, 8 g Total Fat, 1 g Sat Fat, 483 mg Sod, 14 g Total Carb, 5 g Sugar, 7 g Fib, 5 g Prot.

Endive Spears with Chicken Salad and Red Grapefruit

SERVES 6
GLUTEN FREE
NO COOK

---

2 large Belgian endive, separated into leaves

1 red grapefruit

1 cup finely chopped roasted chicken breast

3 tablespoons chopped fresh chives

2 teaspoons olive oil

2 teaspoons champagne vinegar or white-wine vinegar

½ teaspoon salt

⅛ teaspoon black pepper

---

1 Set aside 18 of largest endive leaves. Finely chop enough remaining leaves to equal ⅓ cup. Peel and section grapefruit, making supremes. Chop 8 grapefruit sections; set aside. Reserve any remaining grapefruit for another use.

2 Combine chopped endive, chicken, 2 tablespoons chives, oil, vinegar, salt, and pepper in medium bowl. Mound about 1 tablespoon chicken mixture in each endive leaf. Top leaves evenly with chopped grapefruit and sprinkle with remaining 1 tablespoon chives. Arrange on platter and serve.

Per serving (3 stuffed endive leaves): 101 Cal, 3 g Total Fat, 1 g Sat Fat, 252 mg Sod, 9 g Total Carb, 3 g Sugar, 6 g Fib, 11 g Prot.

Endive Spears with Chicken Salad and Red Grapefruit

Fennel and Carrot Gratin with Pecorino, Orange, and Thyme

 **FENNEL**

Fennel and Carrot Gratin with Pecorino, Orange, and Thyme

SERVES 8
GLUTEN FREE
VEGETARIAN

4 fennel bulbs, trimmed

2 tablespoons olive oil

1½ teaspoons kosher salt

1 pound carrots

3 teaspoons chopped
fresh thyme

3 tablespoons grated
pecorino Romano cheese

1 tablespoon orange juice

1 tablespoon grated
orange zest

1 Preheat oven to 400°F. Spray 8 x 12-inch baking dish with non-stick spray. Line large baking sheet with foil.

2 Cut fennel vertically into ⅓-inch slices (don't worry if some slices break apart); arrange in single layer on prepared baking sheet. Drizzle 1 tablespoon oil evenly over fennel; sprinkle with 1 teaspoon salt and set aside. Cut carrots on diagonal into long ¼-inch slices; put in large bowl and toss well with remaining 1 tablespoon oil and remaining ½ teaspoon salt.

3 Make one layer of fennel in prepared baking dish (use all broken pieces in this layer); sprinkle with 1 teaspoon thyme and 1 tablespoon pecorino. Next, layer all carrots in diagonal rows on top of fennel; sprinkle with 1 teaspoon thyme and 1 tablespoon pecorino. Make another layer of fennel, arranging slices in attractive pattern; sprinkle with remaining 1 teaspoon thyme and remaining 1 tablespoon cheese.

4 Cover dish with foil; roast 30 minutes. Remove foil and roast until vegetables are browned and tender, about 30 minutes longer. Drizzle with orange juice and sprinkle with zest. Cut into 8 servings.

 Per serving (⅛ of gratin): 99 Cal, 4 g Total Fat, 1 g Sat Fat, 499 mg Sod, 14 g Total Carb, 3 g Sugar, 5 g Fib, 2 g Prot.

 **cook's tip**

For a delicious green garnish, save some of the feathery fronds from the top of the fennel bulbs, chop them, and sprinkle them over the gratin just before serving.

Pork Roast Au Poivre with Fennel

SERVES 4
GLUTEN FREE

2 fennel bulbs, trimmed and thinly sliced, fronds chopped

2 tablespoons brandy

1 teaspoon olive oil

1 teaspoon coarse sea salt

2 teaspoons whole black peppercorns, crushed

1 teaspoon fennel seeds, crushed

1 (1¼-pound) lean pork tenderloin, trimmed

1 Preheat oven to 400°F.

2 Put fennel in 9 x 13-inch baking dish. Sprinkle with brandy, oil, and ½ teaspoon salt; toss until mixed well. Arrange fennel in even layer.

3 Stir together peppercorns, fennel seeds, and remaining ½ teaspoon salt in cup; rub all over pork. Place pork on top of fennel; roast until pork is browned and instant-read thermometer inserted into center of pork registers 145°F, 30–35 minutes.

4 Transfer pork to cutting board; let stand 10 minutes. Check fennel; if it is not very tender, return to the oven and continue to roast while pork rests. Cut pork into 12 slices and arrange on serving platter with fennel. Sprinkle with fennel fronds.

Per serving (3 slices pork and ½ cup fennel mixture): 222 Cal, 5 g Total Fat, 1 g Sat Fat, 607 mg Sod, 9 g Total Carb, 0 g Sugar, 4 g Fib, 32 g Prot.

 **GREEN BEANS**

Sautéed Green Beans with Almonds

SERVES 8
GLUTEN FREE
20 MINUTES OR LESS

½ cup slivered almonds

2 teaspoons olive oil

3 garlic cloves, minced

8 cups trimmed green beans

½ cup chicken or vegetable broth

½ teaspoon salt

¼ teaspoon black pepper

 Put almonds in large dry skillet and place over medium heat. Cook, shaking pan frequently, until nuts are golden brown, about 4 minutes. Transfer nuts to plate and let cool.

2 Heat oil in same skillet over medium-high heat. Add garlic and cook, stirring, until fragrant, about 30 seconds. Add green beans and cook, stirring, 1 minute. Add broth and cook, covered, until beans are crisp-tender, about 5 minutes. Sprinkle with salt and pepper. Remove from heat and stir in almonds.

2
SmartPoints value

Per serving (¾ cup): 87 Cal, 5 g Total Fat, 0 g Sat Fat, 200 mg Sod, 10 g Total Carb, 2 g Sugar, 5 g Fib, 4 g Prot.

cook's tip

Try wax beans instead of green beans in this simple, delicous recipe.

Parmesan-Pepper Green Bean Fries

SERVES 6
GLUTEN FREE
VEGETARIAN

2 large egg whites, at room temperature

2 tablespoons water

1 cup grated Parmesan (about 3½ ounces)

1 teaspoon black pepper

12 ounces green beans, trimmed

1 Preheat oven to 425°F. Line large rimmed baking sheet with silicone baking mat or parchment paper.

2 Whisk together egg whites and water in shallow bowl until foamy. In another shallow bowl, mix together Parmesan and pepper.

3 Dip green beans, one at a time, into egg-white mixture; allow excess to drip off. Dip beans into cheese mixture, turning to coat; place on prepared baking sheet about 1 inch apart.

4 Bake until Parmesan melts and browns a little, about 8 minutes. Transfer green beans on baking sheet to wire rack and let cool slightly before serving.

Per serving (10 green bean "fries"): 96 Cal, 5 g Total Fat, 3 g Sat Fat, 277 mg Sod, 5 g Total Carb, 1 g Sugar, 2 g Fib, 9 g Prot.

*Parmesan-Pepper
Green Bean Fries*

Stir-Fried Tempeh with Ginger and Green Beans

SERVES 4
VEGETARIAN
20 MINUTES OR LESS

¾ cup water

3 tablespoons hoisin sauce

2 tablespoons mirin or dry sherry

2 tablespoons soy sauce

2 teaspoons cornstarch

1½ pounds green beans, trimmed

1 tablespoon canola oil

3 tablespoons minced peeled fresh ginger

4 garlic cloves, minced

8 ounces tempeh, diced

1 teaspoon Asian (dark) sesame oil

1 tablespoon sesame seeds, toasted

1 Whisk together water, hoisin, mirin, soy sauce, and cornstarch in small bowl until smooth; set aside.

2 Bring large saucepan of water to boil; add green beans. Return to boil and cook until beans are bright green and crisp-tender, about 4 minutes. Drain.

3 Meanwhile, heat canola oil in wok or large skillet set over medium-high heat. Add ginger and garlic; stir-fry until fragrant, about 1 minute. Stir hoisin mixture again and add to wok along with tempeh. Stir-fry until sauce bubbles and thickens, about 3 minutes. Add green beans and stir-fry until heated through, about 1 minute longer. Stir in sesame oil and sprinkle with sesame seeds.

6 SmartPoints value™

Per serving (1¾ cups): 261 Cal, 12 g Total Fat, 2 g Sat Fat, 646 mg Sod, 27 g Total Carb, 6 g Sugar, 9 g Fib, 15 g Prot.

cook's tip

Brown rice is a healthful and filling side for this tasty stir-fry: ½ cup cooked brown rice per serving will increase the SmartPoints value by 3.

 **JICAMA**

Summer Slaw with Jicama

SERVES 6
GLUTEN FREE
VEGETARIAN
20 MINUTES OR LESS
NO COOK

4 cups lightly packed shredded green cabbage

1½ cups lightly packed shredded peeled jicama

1 cup grated radishes

2 tablespoons lime juice

2 tablespoons rice vinegar

1 teaspoon Asian (dark) sesame oil

½ teaspoon ground cumin

½ teaspoon salt

1 Toss together cabbage, jicama, and radishes in large salad bowl.

2 Add lime juice, vinegar, sesame oil, cumin, and salt; toss until coated evenly.

 Per serving (1 cup): 40 Cal, 1 g Total Fat, 0 g Sat Fat, 214 mg Sod, 8 g Total Carb, 3 g Sugar, 3 g Fib, 1 g Prot.

*Jicama-Ham Hash Browns
with Fried Eggs*

Jicama-Ham Hash Browns with Fried Eggs

SERVES 4
GLUTEN FREE

3 ounces Canadian
bacon, diced

1 teaspoon olive oil

4 cups peeled, shredded
jicama, squeezed dry

2 cups diced onion

1 teaspoon granulated garlic

¾ teaspoon kosher salt

½ teaspoon smoked paprika

⅛ teaspoon black pepper

4 large eggs

1 tablespoon chopped
fresh parsley

1 Spray large skillet with nonstick spray and heat over medium-high heat. Add bacon and cook, stirring often, until lightly browned, about 5 minutes. Remove bacon from pan; set aside.

2 Add oil, jicama, onion, garlic, salt, paprika, and pepper to same skillet. Increase heat to high; cook, stirring often, until onion is softened and jicama begins to brown, 10–12 minutes. Transfer jicama mixture to bowl; add Canadian bacon and gently stir to combine. Cover to keep warm.

3 Wipe skillet clean. Off heat, spray with nonstick spray and set over medium heat. Fry eggs. Divide hash evenly among 4 plates; top each with 1 fried egg. Sprinkle with parsley.

Per serving (1 egg and ⅔ cup hash): 184 Cal, 7 g Total Fat, 2 g Sat Fat, 597 mg Sod, 19 g Total Carb, 6 g Sugar, 7 g Fib, 12 g Prot.

KALE

Shaved kale Salad with Pecorino Romano

SERVES 4
GLUTEN FREE
VEGETARIAN
20 MINUTES OR LESS
NO COOK

2 tablespoons lemon juice

2 teaspoons extra-virgin olive oil

¼ teaspoon salt

⅛ teaspoon black pepper

2 (¾-pound) bunches Tuscan (Lacinato) kale, ribs removed and leaves very thinly sliced

3 radishes, thinly sliced

6 tablespoons shredded pecorino Romano

2 tablespoons toasted pine nuts

1 To make dressing, whisk together lemon juice, oil, salt, and pepper in large bowl. Add kale and toss until coated evenly. Let stand at room temperature, tossing occasionally, 10 minutes.

2 Add radishes and toss. Divide kale mixture evenly among 4 plates. Sprinkle each salad with 1½ tablespoons pecorino and ½ tablespoon pine nuts.

 Per serving (2 cups kale, 1½ tablespoons cheese, and ½ tablespoon nuts): 162 Cal, 8 g Fat, 2 g Sat Fat, 370 g Sod, 18 g Total Carb, O g Sugar, 4 g Fib, 8 g Prot.

cook's tip For a hearty, very Italian salad, you can top each serving with 1 ounce thinly sliced prosciutto, cut into strips. The per-serving SmartPoints value will increase by 3.

Shaved Kale Salad
with Pecorino Romano

Minestrone with Kale

SERVES 8
VEGETARIAN

2 teaspoons olive oil

2 zucchini, quartered
lengthwise and cut
into ¼-inch slices

10 baby-cut carrots, halved

1 onion, chopped

3 cups lightly packed coarsely
chopped trimmed kale

1 (28-ounce) can diced
tomatoes with basil, garlic,
and oregano

4 cups reduced-sodium
vegetable broth

1 (15-ounce) can great
northern beans, rinsed
and drained

⅓ cup orzo

¼ teaspoon salt

¼ teaspoon black pepper

¾ cup grated Parmesan

1 Heat oil in large pot over medium heat. Add zucchini, carrots, and onion; cook, stirring, until onion is softened, about 5 minutes. Add kale and cook, stirring, until wilted, about 5 minutes.

2 Add tomatoes, broth, beans, and orzo. Simmer until carrots and orzo are tender, about 15 minutes. Stir in salt and pepper. Ladle soup evenly into 8 bowls and sprinkle with Parmesan.

Per serving (1 cup soup with 1½ tablespoons Parmesan): 191 Cal, 5 g Total Fat, 2 g Sat Fat, 480 mg Sod, 28 g Total Carb, 6 g Sugar, 5 g Fib, 11 g Prot.

cook's tip

The addition of kale gives this minestrone a bold earthy flavor and a nutritional boost.

Slow-Cooked Sausage, Kale, Shrimp, and Black-Eyed Peas

SERVES 8
GLUTEN FREE

1 teaspoon olive oil

½ pound hot Italian turkey sausage, casings removed

1 sweet onion, such as Vidalia, chopped

3 garlic cloves, minced

1 tablespoon smoked paprika

1 teaspoon dried oregano

1 (¾-pound) bunch kale, trimmed and coarsely chopped

1 (28-ounce) can crushed tomatoes

2 (15½-ounce) cans black-eyed peas, rinsed and drained

2 cups chicken broth

1 pound large shrimp, peeled and deveined

½ cup sliced roasted red peppers (not oil-packed)

1 Heat oil in large heavy nonstick skillet over medium-high heat. Add sausage and cook, breaking it up with wooden spoon, until lightly browned, about 4 minutes. Transfer sausage to a 5- to 6-quart slow cooker.

2 Add onion to skillet; cover and cook, stirring occasionally, until golden, about 8 minutes. Stir in garlic, paprika, and oregano; cook, stirring, until fragrant, about 30 seconds. Add kale; cover and cook, stirring occasionally, until wilted, about 4 minutes.

3 Transfer kale mixture to slow cooker. Stir in tomatoes, black-eyed peas, and broth. Cover and cook until kale is very tender, 3–4 hours on high or 6–8 hours on low.

4 Add shrimp and roasted red peppers to slow cooker; mix well. Cover and cook on high until the shrimp are opaque in center, about 20 minutes longer.

Per serving (1½ cups): 289 Cal, 6 g Total Fat, 1 g Sat Fat, 891 mg Sod, 32 g Total Carb, 5 g Sugar, 8 g Fib, 29 g Prot.

Bibb Lettuce, Cucumber, and Radish Salad

SERVES 4
GLUTEN FREE
VEGETARIAN
20 MINUTES OR LESS
NO COOK

1 head Bibb lettuce,
leaves separated

½ English (seedless)
cucumber, halved lengthwise
and thinly sliced

2 radishes, thinly sliced

2 tablespoons white-wine
vinegar

1½ tablespoons olive oil

1½ tablespoons minced shallot

2 teaspoons water

1 teaspoon honey

¼ teaspoon salt

⅛ teaspoon black pepper

4 tablespoons slivered
almonds, toasted

1 Place one fourth of lettuce leaves on each of 4 plates; top each with one fourth of cucumber and one fourth of radishes.

2 To make dressing, whisk together vinegar, oil, shallot, water, honey, salt, and pepper in small bowl until blended. Drizzle about 1 tablespoon dressing over each salad and sprinkle each with 1 tablespoon almonds.

Per serving (1 salad with 1 tablespoon almonds): 107 Cal, 9 g Total Fat, 1 g Sat Fat, 150 mg Sod, 7 g Total Carb, 3 g Sugar, 2 g Fib, 2 g Prot.

Bibb Lettuce, Cucumber, and Radish Salad

Chilled Green Gazpacho

SERVES 4
VEGETARIAN
NO COOK

Combine all ingredients in food processor or in batches in blender and puree. Refrigerate until chilled, at least 1 hour or up to 1 day.

2 cups lightly packed chopped romaine lettuce

1 cup peeled and chopped English (seedless) cucumber

1 cup chopped celery

1 cup seedless green grapes

¾ cup vegetable broth

4 scallions, chopped

1 slice white bread, crusts removed, bread diced

1 tablespoon red-wine vinegar or sherry vinegar

½ teaspoon salt

¼ teaspoon black pepper

Per serving (about 1 cup): 63 Cal, 0 g Total Fat, 0 g Sat Fat, 536 mg Sod, 14 g Total Carb, 8 g Sugar, 2 g Fib, 2 g Prot.

cook's tip

This unusual combination of lettuce, cucumber, and grapes results in a sweet, refreshing soup that's packed with nutrition.

Ginger-Teriyaki Chicken in Romaine

SERVES 4

1 cup chicken broth

1 tablespoon minced peeled
fresh ginger

1 garlic clove, minced

1 pound skinless boneless
chicken breasts, cut into
bite-size pieces

1 celery stalk, cut into
small dice

1 small red bell pepper, cut
into small dice

1 scallion, green part only,
finely chopped

¼ cup teriyaki sauce

¼ teaspoon black pepper

16 inner romaine
lettuce leaves

1 Combine broth, ginger, and garlic in large skillet; bring to simmer. Add chicken and return to simmer. Cover and simmer until chicken is cooked through, about 15 minutes. Remove from heat and let chicken cool in broth.

2 Spoon 3 tablespoons of ginger broth into medium bowl; save remaining broth for another use. Add chicken, celery, bell pepper, scallion, teriyaki sauce, and black pepper to bowl; stir until mixed well.

3 To serve, arrange 4 lettuce leaves on each of 4 plates. Spoon ¼ cup chicken mixture into each leaf. Pick up each leaf to eat out of hand.

Per serving (4 filled lettuce leaves): 190 Cal, 5 g Total Fat, 1 g Sat Fat, 949 mg Sod, 9 g Total Carb, 3 g Sugar, 3 g Fib, 30 g Prot.

Creole-Style Stuffed Mushrooms

SERVES 8
VEGETARIAN

24 large white mushrooms (about 1 pound)

1 teaspoon olive oil

¼ cup finely chopped onion

¼ cup finely chopped red bell pepper

1 (10-ounce) package frozen chopped spinach, thawed and squeezed dry

2½ slices whole wheat bread, made into crumbs

1 teaspoon Creole or Cajun seasoning

¼ teaspoon ground turmeric

1 Preheat oven to 350°F. Lightly spray large rimmed baking sheet with nonstick spray.

2 Pull out mushroom stems and finely chop; reserve caps.

3 Heat oil in large skillet over high heat. Add mushroom stems, onion, bell pepper, and spinach; cook, stirring, until mushroom stems and onion are softened, about 5 minutes. Remove skillet from heat and stir in bread crumbs, Creole seasoning, and ground turmeric

4 Stuff each mushroom cap with about 2 tablespoons spinach mixture. Place mushrooms stuffed sides up on prepared baking sheet. Bake until heated through and mushroom caps are tender, about 15 minutes; serve warm.

Per serving (3 mushrooms): 53 Cal, 1 g Total Fat, 0 g Sat Fat, 163 mg Sod, 8 g Total Carb, 2 g Sugar, 3 g Fib, 1 g Prot.

Mushroom Barley Risotto

SERVES 6
VEGETARIAN

5 cups vegetable broth

2 teaspoons olive oil

12 ounces mixed wild
mushrooms, trimmed
and sliced

2 carrots, diced

2 shallots, finely chopped

2 garlic cloves, finely chopped

1½ cups quick-cooking barley

¼ cup grated Parmesan

1 tablespoon unsalted butter

¼ teaspoon salt

2 tablespoons chopped
fresh parsley

1 Bring broth to boil in medium saucepan. Reduce heat and keep at simmer.

2 Meanwhile, heat oil in large saucepan over medium-high heat. Add mushrooms, carrots, shallots, and garlic. Cook, stirring frequently, until vegetables are softened, about 5 minutes. Add barley and cook, stirring, 1 minute. Add 1 cup broth. Cook, stirring occasionally, until broth is absorbed. Add remaining broth, about ¾ cup at a time, stirring frequently until it is absorbed before adding more. Cook until barley is tender, 25–30 minutes longer.

3 Remove pan from heat. Stir in Parmesan, butter, and salt until mixed well. Spoon into large serving bowl. Sprinkle with parsley.

 8 SmartPoints value

Per serving (1 cup): 263 Cal, 5 g Total Fat, 2 g Sat Fat, 983 mg Sod, 47 g Total Carb, 4 g Sugar, 9 g Fib, 9 g Prot.

cook's tip

A mix of mushrooms gives this grain dish visual and textural appeal, but you could also use a single flavorful variety such as shiitakes or oyster mushrooms.

Tofu "Steaks"
with Onions
and Mushrooms

Tofu "Steaks" with Onions and Mushrooms

SERVES 4
GLUTEN FREE
VEGETARIAN

4 teaspoons olive oil

2 onions, thinly sliced

½ pound cremini or white mushrooms, sliced

1 teaspoon fresh thyme leaves

3 teaspoons steak seasoning

1 (14-ounce) package extra-firm tofu, drained

¼ teaspoon salt

1 Heat 2 teaspoons oil in large nonstick skillet over medium heat. Add onions and cook, stirring frequently, until lightly browned, about 8 minutes. Add mushrooms, thyme, and 1 teaspoon steak seasoning. Cook, stirring frequently, until mushrooms are tender, about 5 minutes.

2 Meanwhile, brush ridged grill pan with remaining 2 teaspoons oil and set over medium heat.

3 Cut tofu lengthwise in half, and then cut crosswise in half to make 4 "steaks." Sprinkle with remaining 2 teaspoons steak seasoning and salt. Place tofu in grill pan and cook until browned and heated through, about 3 minutes per side. Serve topped with onions and mushrooms.

Per serving (1 piece tofu and ½ cup vegetables): 174 Cal, 10 g Total Fat, 1 g Sat Fat, 199 mg Sod, 11 g Total Carb, 4 g Sugar, 4 g Fib, 13 g Prot.

Slow-Cooker French Onion Soup

SERVES 6

3 pounds Spanish, white, or
yellow onions, sliced

2 tablespoons unsalted
butter, melted

2 teaspoons salt

¼ cup dry sherry

1 garlic clove, minced

3 cups reduced-sodium
chicken broth

3 cups reduced-sodium
beef broth

1 teaspoon sugar

5 fresh thyme sprigs plus
1 tablespoon chopped
thyme leaves

1 bay leaf

1 teaspoon reduced-sodium
soy sauce

¼ teaspoon black pepper

3 tablespoons grated
Parmesan cheese

1 Combine onions, butter, and salt in slow cooker. Cover and cook until onions are well browned, 8–10 hours on high. Add sherry and garlic, stirring to combine. Cook, uncovered, to allow alcohol to burn off, about 10 minutes on high.

2 Stir in chicken broth, beef broth, sugar, thyme sprigs, and bay leaf; cover and cook 2–3 hours on high to allow flavors to blend. Remove and discard thyme sprigs and bay leaf; stir in soy sauce and pepper. Ladle soup evenly into 6 soup bowls; sprinkle each serving with 1½ teaspoons Parmesan and chopped thyme.

Per serving (1½ cups soup and 1½ teaspoons Parmesan): 167 Cal, 5 g Total Fat, 3 g Sat Fat, 1,245 mg Sod, 23 g Total Carb, 11 g Sugar, 4 g Fib, 5 g Prot.

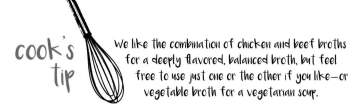

cook's tip

We like the combination of chicken and beef broths for a deeply flavored, balanced broth, but feel free to use just one or the other if you like—or vegetable broth for a vegetarian soup.

 **PARSNIPS**

Parsnip and Pear Puree

SERVES 6
GLUTEN FREE
VEGETARIAN

4 parsnips, peeled and diced

3 ripe pears, halved, cored, and diced

¼ cup water

3 tablespoons low-fat buttermilk

⅛ teaspoon ground cardamom

¼ teaspoon salt

¼ teaspoon black pepper

1 Combine parsnips, pears, and water in large saucepan; bring to boil. Reduce heat to low and simmer, covered, until parsnips are very tender, about 15 minutes, adding water if mixture seems dry. Drain off any liquid.

2 Transfer parsnip mixture to blender or food processor. Add buttermilk, cardamom, salt, and pepper and pulse until coarse puree is formed. Reheat if necessary.

 Per serving (about ½ cup): 132 Cal, 0 g Total Fat, 0 g Sat Fat, 116 mg Sod, 32 g Total Carb, 14 g Sugar, 8 g Fib, 2 g Prot.

Roasted Parsnips and Carrots

SERVES 8
GLUTEN FREE
VEGETARIAN

8 carrots, halved or quartered lengthwise and cut into 2-inch lengths

6 parsnips, peeled, halved or quartered lengthwise

1 tablespoon minced fresh thyme

1 teaspoon kosher salt

½ teaspoon black pepper

1 tablespoon olive oil

1 Preheat oven to 400°F. Spray large nonstick rimmed baking sheet with nonstick spray.

2 Combine carrots and parsnips on prepared baking sheet; sprinkle with thyme, salt, and pepper. Drizzle with oil and toss until coated evenly. Arange vegetables to form single layer. Roast 20 minutes; turn vegetables over and roast until they start to caramelize, 15–20 minutes longer.

Per serving (about ⅔ cup): 131 Cal, 2 g Total Fat, 0 g Sat Fat, 295 mg Sod, 28 g Total Carb, 9 g Sugar, 8 g Fib, 2 g Prot.

cook's tip

Either chopped parsley, thyme, or tarragon would make an excellent fresh garnish for these root vegetables.

PEAS

Green Pea Dip

SERVES 8
GLUTEN FREE
VEGETARIAN

10 ounces (about 1½ cups)
fresh or frozen green peas

1 tablespoon olive oil

1 tablespoon fresh lime juice

¾ teaspoon ground cumin

½ teaspoon salt

1 plum tomato, seeded
and diced

2 tablespoons finely chopped
red onion

3 tablespoons chopped fresh
cilantro leaves

¼ teaspoon hot pepper sauce,
or to taste

1 Bring small saucepan half filled with water to boil. Add peas; adjust heat and simmer until peas are very tender, 4–5 minutes. Drain and cool under cold running water. Drain again.

2 Put peas, oil, lime juice, cumin, and salt in food processor and puree. Scrape into bowl and stir in tomato, onion, cilantro, and pepper sauce. Cover and refrigerate at least 15 minutes or up to 1 day for flavors to blend.

 Per serving (about 3 tablespoons): 48 Cal, 2 g Total Fat, 0 g Sat Fat, 153 mg Sod, 6 g Total Carb, 3 g Sugar, 2 g Fib, 2 g Prot.

Lemony Sugar Snap Pea Salad

SERVES 4
GLUTEN FREE
VEGETARIAN
20 MINUTES OR LESS

½ pound sugar snap peas
(about 2 cups), trimmed

2 tablespoons lemon juice

1½ tablespoons olive oil

¼ teaspoon salt

⅛ teaspoon black pepper

2 Kirby cucumbers, halved
lengthwise and thinly sliced

¼ cup crumbled feta

3 tablespoons chopped
fresh chives

3 tablespoons thinly sliced
fresh mint leaves

---

1 Bring large saucepan of water to boil. Add snap peas and cook until just bright green and crisp-tender, 1–2 minutes. Drain and rinse under cold running water; drain again. Thinly slice snap peas lengthwise.

2 To make dressing, whisk together lemon juice, oil, salt, and pepper in medium salad bowl. Add snap peas, cucumbers, feta, chives, and mint; toss until mixed.

Per serving (about 1 cup): 98 Cal, 7 g Total Fat, 2 g Sat Fat, 252 mg Sod, 7 g Total Carb, 2 g Sugar, 2 g Fib, 3 g Prot.

Lemony Sugar Snap Pea Salad

Cheddar Fries

SERVES 4
GLUTEN FREE
VEGETARIAN

2 (9-ounce) russet potatoes

¼ teaspoon salt

¼ teaspoon black pepper

⅓ cup shredded reduced-fat sharp Cheddar

1 Preheat oven to 400°F. Line large rimmed baking sheet with silicone baking mat or parchment paper. (If your baking sheet is nonstick you can leave it unlined.)

2 Peel potatoes and cut into ¼-inch-wide strips (you should have about 52). Place on prepared baking sheet. Spray with nonstick spray, sprinkle with salt and pepper, and toss until coated evenly. Arrange potatoes to form single layer, making sure potatoes do not touch or overlap.

3 Bake 20 minutes. Turn fries over and spread out. Bake until golden brown, about 20 minutes longer.

4 Gather fries together; sprinkle with Cheddar. Bake until cheese is melted, about 5 minutes. Transfer fries in pan to wire rack and let cool several minutes before serving.

3 SmartPoints value™ **Per serving** (about 13 fries). 123 Cal, 1 g Total Fat, 1 g Sat Fat, 239 mg Sod, 22 g Total Carb, 1 g Sugar, 3 g Fib, 6 g Prot.

Cheddar Fries

Italian Potato Torta with Spinach and Cheese

SERVES 6
VEGETARIAN

1½ pounds small Yukon Gold potatoes

2 tablespoons Italian-seasoned dried bread crumbs

2 teaspoons olive oil

4 garlic cloves, minced

1 (6-ounce) package baby spinach

2 large eggs

½ cup fat-free milk

¼ teaspoon salt

¼ teaspoon ground nutmeg

⅛ teaspoon black pepper

1 cup shredded reduced-fat Italian cheese blend

¼ cup grated Parmesan cheese

1 Place potatoes and enough lightly salted water to cover in medium saucepan. Bring to boil and cook until tender, about 20 minutes; drain. Transfer to large bowl and mash until smooth.

2 Preheat oven to 375°F. Spray 9-inch pie plate with nonstick spray; sprinkle with bread crumbs to coat bottom and side of plate.

3 Meanwhile, heat oil in large nonstick skillet over medium heat. Add garlic and cook, stirring constantly, until fragrant, about 30 seconds. Add spinach and cook, stirring, until wilted, about 2 minutes. Add spinach mixture to potatoes, stirring to combine. Let cool slightly.

4 Whisk together eggs, milk, salt, nutmeg, and pepper in medium bowl. Stir in Italian cheese blend. Stir egg mixture into potato mixture; spoon into prepared pie plate.

5 Bake until torta is heated through and lightly browned, about 25 minutes. Sprinkle with Parmesan. Bake until cheese is melted, about 3 minutes longer. Cool 5 minutes and cut into 6 wedges.

Per serving (1 wedge): 208 Cal, 8 g Total Fat, 3 g Sat Fat, 396 mg Sod, 23 g Total Carb, 3 g Sugar, 4 g Fib, 12 g Prot.

cook's tip

If you like, add 1 cup of sliced white or cremini mushrooms to the skillet along with the spinach in step 3, and cook until tender, about 6 minutes, with no change in the SmartPoints value.

 **RADISHES**

Blackened Tilapia with Radish-Cucumber Salsa

SERVES 4
GLUTEN FREE
20 MINUTES OR LESS

5 radishes, halved and thinly sliced crosswise

1 large Kirby cucumber, diced

½ red bell pepper, diced

3 scallions, sliced

1 tablespoon chopped fresh cilantro

2 tablespoons lime juice

⅛ teaspoon salt

⅛ teaspoon black pepper

2 teaspoons olive oil

4 (6-ounce) tilapia fillets

2 tablespoons blackened seasoning

1 Mix together radishes, cucumber, bell pepper, scallions, cilantro, lime juice, salt, black pepper, and 1 teaspoon oil in medium bowl.

2 Heat remaining 1 teaspoon oil in large nonstick skillet over medium-high heat. Sprinkle tilapia with blackened seasoning and add fish to skillet in single layer (cook in batches if necessary). Cook until just opaque in center, about 3 minutes per side.

3 Place 1 fish fillet on each of 4 plates. Top evenly with salsa.

 Per serving (1 fillet with ½ cup salsa): 179 Cal, 4 g Total Fat, 1 g Sat Fat, 139 mg Sod, 5 g Total Carb, 1 g Sugar, 1 g Fib, 32 g Prot.

*Rosemary Roasted
Radishes with Greens*

Rosemary Roasted Radishes with Greens

SERVES 4
GLUTEN FREE
VEGETARIAN

2 large bunches radishes with green tops attached (about 20 radishes)

1 tablespoon olive oil

2 teaspoons chopped fresh rosemary

½ teaspoon salt

¼ teaspoon black pepper

1 teaspoon lemon juice

1 Preheat oven to 425°F. Position a rack in top third of oven.

2 Separate radishes and radish greens; set greens aside. Rinse radishes and trim root if necessary. Cut radishes in half.

3 Combine radishes, olive oil, rosemary, salt, and pepper in large bowl, tossing until well coated. Transfer to large rimmed baking sheet, leaving about ½ to 1 teaspoon oil mixture in bowl. Place radishes in top third of oven.

4 While radishes roast, rinse greens several times in cold water to remove grit. Discard any wilted, browned, or yellow leaves. Tear any large leaves in half and remove any tough stems. Place greens in bowl and toss to coat in remaining olive-oil mixture.

5 After 20 minutes of roasting, carefully remove pan from oven. Add greens to baking sheet and toss to combine. Roast until greens wilt and radishes are tender, about 5 minutes longer. Drizzle with lemon juice.

Per serving (generous ⅔ cup): 35 Cal, 3 g Total Fat, 0 g Sat Fat, 301 mg Sod, 1 g Total Carb, 1 g Sugar, 1 g Fib, 0 g Prot.

Bahn Mi-Style Roast Beef Subs with Pickled Daikon

SERVES 4
NO COOK

⅓ cup rice vinegar

2 tablespoons sugar

¼ teaspoon salt

2 tablespoons water

1 cup matchstick-cut or shredded daikon radish

2 slices white onion, halved and separated

¼ red bell pepper, cut into very thin strips

1 (12-ounce) soft French baguette

¼ cup reduced-fat mayonnaise

2 teaspoons Sriracha

½ cup shredded carrot

8 (1-ounce) slices deli-style lean sirloin roast beef

½ cup small sprigs fresh cilantro

1 Combine vinegar, sugar, salt, and water in large bowl and stir until sugar dissolves. Stir in daikon, onion, and bell pepper. Cover and refrigerate 15–30 minutes, stirring occasionally. (May be made up to 1 day ahead.)

2 Slice baguette lengthwise, almost all the way through. Scoop out soft interior of bread and discard, or save for another use. Stir mayonnaise and Sriracha together in small cup; spread evenly on inside of baguette. Layer carrot and roast beef evenly into baguette. Drain vegetables and place over beef and top with cilantro. Cut into 4 sandwiches.

Per serving (1 sandwich): 307 Cal, 9 g Total Fat, 2 g Sat Fat, 1,034 mg Sod, 34 g Total Carb, 5 g Sugar, 2 g Fib, 19 g Prot.

Bacon, Egg, and Spinach Breakfast Stacks

SERVES 6
GLUTEN FREE

3 very small red or new potatoes (about 6 ounces), scrubbed

5 ounces baby spinach

½ cup part-skim ricotta

1 large egg, lightly beaten

1 tablespoon chopped fresh chives

3 thin slices Canadian bacon, quartered

½ cup shredded reduced-fat Cheddar

1 Preheat oven to 350°F. Line 6 cups of muffin pan with paper liners.

2 Combine potatoes with enough water to cover in medium saucepan; bring to boil. Cook until almost cooked through, about 10 minutes; drain and let cool. Slice each potato into 4 rounds; set aside.

3 Bring 1 inch water to boil in large pot. Add spinach; cook, covered, until just wilted, about 3 minutes. Drain spinach and let cool; squeeze out any excess water and set spinach aside.

4 Mix together ricotta, egg, and chives in small bowl.

5 Place middle slice of potato in bottom of each prepared muffin cup. Top each with 1 piece bacon, heaping 1 teaspoon ricotta mixture, about 2 tablespoons spinach, about 1 tablespoon Cheddar cheese, another piece bacon, and another heaping 1 teaspoon ricotta mixture. Top each stack with potato slice and sprinkle evenly with remaining Cheddar.

6 Bake stacks until set, 30–35 minutes. Let cool in muffin pan about 10 minutes; serve, or remove and place on wire rack to cool completely.

2 SmartPoints value™

Per serving (1 stack): 97 Cal, 4 g Total Fat, 2 g Sat Fat, 224 mg Sod, 7 g Total Carb, 1 g Sugar, 1 g Fib, 10 g Prot.

cook's tip

These tasty stacks can be prepared ahead of time, refrigerated up to 4 days, and reheated in the microwave.

*Braised Mixed Greens
over Creamy Polenta*

Braised Mixed Greens over Creamy Polenta

SERVES 4
GLUTEN FREE
VEGETARIAN

2 teaspoons olive oil

1 small onion, thinly sliced

3 garlic cloves, thinly sliced

½ head escarole, chopped

½ cup dry red wine

6 ounces baby spinach

1 bunch Swiss chard (about 1 pound), stems removed and thinly sliced, leaves chopped

2 teaspoons chopped fresh thyme

2 tablespoons capers, chopped

½ teaspoon salt

1 cup low-fat (1%) milk

1 cup vegetable broth

½ cup instant polenta

1 Heat oil in large skillet over medium heat. Add onion and cook, stirring occasionally, until softened, about 5 minutes. Add garlic and cook, stirring constantly, until fragrant, about 30 seconds. Stir in escarole and wine; cook, covered, 5 minutes. Stir in spinach, Swiss chard leaves and stems, thyme, capers, and ¼ teaspoon salt. Cook, covered, until greens are tender, 8–10 minutes.

2 Meanwhile, to make polenta, combine milk, broth, and remaining ¼ teaspoon salt in medium saucepan; bring to boil over medium-high heat. Add polenta in thin, steady stream, whisking constantly. Cook, stirring constantly with wooden spoon, until thick and creamy, about 5 minutes. Divide polenta evenly among 4 large shallow bowls; top evenly with greens.

 Per serving (½ cup polenta and ¾ cup greens): 195 Cal, 3 g Total Fat, 1 g Sat Fat, 903 mg Sod, 30 g Total Carb, 6 g Sugar, 7 g Fib, 8 g Prot.

cook's tip Using a mixture of spinach and other greens and braising them in red wine adds layers of flavor to this simple dish. Vary the greens depending on what you find at the market.

Sautéed Spinach with Crispy Garlic

SERVES 6
GLUTEN FREE
VEGETARIAN
20 MINUTES OR LESS

---

1 tablespoon olive oil

4 large garlic cloves, thinly sliced lengthwise

2 pounds baby spinach

½ teaspoon salt

¼ teaspoon red pepper flakes

---

1 Heat oil in large nonstick skillet over medium heat. Add garlic and cook, tossing occasionally, until light golden, about 2½ minutes. With slotted spoon, transfer garlic to plate.

2 Add spinach to skillet in batches, and cook, tossing with tongs, until spinach wilts, about 2 minutes per batch, transferring each batch to serving bowl.

3 Return spinach to skillet (discard any liquid in bowl) and sprinkle with salt and pepper flakes; toss until mixed well. Return spinach to bowl; sprinkle with garlic and toss.

Per serving (about ⅔ cup): 58 Cal, 3 g Total Fat, 0 g Sat Fat, 314 mg Sod, 6 g Total Carb, 1 g Sugar, 4 g Fib, 4 g Prot.

cook's tip

To keep the garlic crispy, toss it with the spinach just before serving.

Summer Vegetable Lasagna with Plum Tomatoes

SERVES 6
VEGETARIAN

1 (15-ounce) container part-skim ricotta cheese

1 large egg white, lightly beaten

1 (16-ounce) package frozen chopped spinach, thawed and squeezed dry

½ cup shredded reduced-fat Italian cheese blend

1 teaspoon salt

¼ teaspoon red pepper flakes

2 zucchini, cut lengthwise into strips with vegetable peeler

2½ cups marinara sauce

6 (3 x 7-inch) no-boil whole wheat lasagna noodles

4 plum tomatoes, sliced

1 small onion, thinly sliced

1 Preheat oven to 400°F. Spray 8-inch square baking dish with nonstick spray.

2 Stir together ricotta and egg white in medium bowl. Stir in spinach, cheese blend, ½ teaspoon salt, and red pepper flakes.

3 Toss together zucchini strips and remaining ½ teaspoon salt in large bowl.

4 Spread about one-third of sauce over bottom of prepared baking dish. Top with 2 lasagna noodles. Top noodles with half of zucchini, half of ricotta mixture, half of plum tomatoes, half of onion, and half of remaining sauce. Repeat layering beginning with 2 lasagna noodles, remaining ricotta mixture, remaining plum tomatoes, and remaining onion. Top with remaining 2 lasagna noodles and remaining sauce.

5 Cover baking dish with foil and bake 40 minutes. Uncover and bake until lasagna is bubbly, about 15 minutes longer. Let stand 10 minutes before serving.

8 SmartPoints value

Per serving (⅙ of lasagna): 303 Cal, 11 g Total Fat, 5 g Sat Fat, 999 mg Sod, 34 g Total Carb, 11 g Sugar, 6 g Fib, 18 g Prot.

Cherry Tomatoes Stuffed with Feta and Cucumber

SERVES 12
GLUTEN FREE
VEGETARIAN
20 MINUTES OR LESS
NO COOK

24 cherry tomatoes

¼ cup light cream cheese (Neufchâtel), at room temperature

3 tablespoons crumbled feta

1 tablespoon reduced-calorie mayonnaise

⅛ teaspoon black pepper

¼ cup finely diced English (seedless) cucumber

2 tablespoons finely chopped scallion, plus additional for garnish

2 teaspoons chopped fresh dill, plus additional for garnish

1 Cut off top of each tomato. Using melon baller or tip of small spoon, scoop out seeds.

2 Stir together cream cheese, feta, mayonnaise, and pepper in small bowl; stir in cucumber, scallion, and dill. Spoon cheese mixture into small zip-close plastic bag; snip off one corner of bag and pipe mixture evenly into tomatoes.

3 Arrange tomatoes on serving platter; sprinkle with additional scallion and dill. Refrigerate until chilled, at least 30 minutes or up to 4 hours.

Per serving (2 stuffed tomatoes): 27 Cal, 2 g Total Fat, 1 g Sat Fat, 60 mg Sod, 2 g Total Carb, 1 g Sugar, 0 g Fib, 1 g Prot.

cook's tip

To ensure that the tomatoes stand securely, cut a thin slice off the bottom of each one.

Cherry Tomatoes Stuffed with Feta and Cucumber

Quick-Cook
Tomato Sauce

Quick-Cook Tomato Sauce

SERVES 8
GLUTEN FREE
VEGETARIAN
20 MINUTES OR LESS

3 tablespoons olive oil

1 small onion, chopped

4 large garlic cloves, minced

*2 pounds ripe tomatoes,
cored and diced*

1 tablespoon tomato paste

2 teaspoons kosher salt

½ cup chopped fresh basil

1 Heat oil in large saucepan over medium heat. Add onion and cook, stirring, until softened, about 5 minutes. Add garlic and cook, stirring frequently, until fragrant, about 30 seconds.

2 Add tomatoes with their juice, tomato paste, and salt; cook, stirring, until tomatoes break down and begin to soften, 4–5 minutes. Stir in basil.

Per serving (½ cup): 72 Cal, 5 g Total Fat, 1 g Sat Fat, 505 mg Sod, 6 g Total Carb, 4 g Sugar, 2 g Fib, 1 g Prot.

cook's tip

This sauce is excellent over pasta, but also try it as a topping for spaghetti squash, grilled eggplant, or chicken breasts, or in casseroles.

Roasted Acorn Squash with Thyme

SERVES 4
GLUTEN FREE
VEGETARIAN

2 acorn squash

1 tablespoon olive oil

1½ tablespoons chopped fresh thyme

½ teaspoon kosher salt

¼ teaspoon black pepper

1 Preheat oven to 400°F. Spray large rimmed baking sheet with nonstick spray.

2 Halve squash, scrape out seeds with spoon, and cut halves again so you have total of 8 wedges. Place squash wedges skin side down on prepared baking sheet. Brush with oil; sprinkle with thyme, salt, and pepper. Roast until squash are tender and golden along edges, about 40 minutes.

Per serving (2 wedges): 118 Cal, 4 g Total Fat, 1 g Sat Fat, 248 mg Sod, 23 g Total Carb, 0 g Sugar, 3 g Fib, 2 g Prot.

cook's tip You can also substitute other small winter squash for acorn, including carnival or delicata squash.

Greek-Style Spaghetti Squash

SERVES 4
GLUTEN FREE
VEGETARIAN

1 (2-pound) spaghetti squash

2 teaspoons olive oil

3 scallions, sliced

1 large garlic clove, minced

1 (14½-ounce) can diced tomatoes

1 cup canned chickpeas, rinsed and drained

1 teaspoon dried oregano

1 teaspoon grated lemon zest

¼ teaspoon salt

¼ teaspoon black pepper

¼ cup chopped fresh dill or mint, or a combination

¼ cup crumbled reduced-fat feta

1 With tines of fork, pierce squash in several places; place on microwavable plate. Microwave on High, turning squash over every 3 minutes, until tender, 12–15 minutes; let stand 5 minutes. Cut squash lengthwise in half and scrape out seeds.

2 Meanwhile, heat oil in large nonstick skillet over medium heat. Add scallions and garlic; cook, stirring, until fragrant, about 1 minute. Add tomatoes, chickpeas, oregano, lemon zest, salt, and pepper; increase heat to high and bring to boil. Remove from heat.

3 Using fork, scrape spaghetti-like squash strands from squash. Stir into tomato-chickpea mixture and set over medium heat. Cook, stirring, until mixed well; remove from heat and stir in dill. Divide evenly among 4 large bowls; sprinkle with feta.

3 SmartPoints value™

Per serving (about 1 cup squash mixture and 1 tablespoon cheese): 184 Cal, 5 g Total Fat, 1 g Sat Fat, 561 mg Sod, 31 g Total Carb, 3 g Sugar, 5 g Fib, 7 g Prot.

cook's tip

To bake the squash instead of microwaving it, halve it and scoop out the seeds. Place cut side down in a large baking dish, add ½ cup water to dish, and bake at 350°F until tender, 30–40 minutes.

Coconut-Curry Butternut Squash Soup

SERVES 8
GLUTEN FREE

4 pounds butternut squash, peeled, seeded, and cut into 1-inch cubes (about 8½ cups)

1 tablespoon canola oil

2 onions, chopped

2 garlic cloves, minced

1 tablespoon grated peeled fresh ginger

1 tablespoon curry powder, preferably Madras

2 cups reduced-sodium chicken broth

1 (13½-ounce) can light (low-fat) coconut milk

1 teaspoon kosher salt

⅛ teaspoon cayenne

1 tablespoon lime juice

2 scallions, thinly sliced diagonally

2 tablespoons finely chopped fresh cilantro

1 Preheat oven to 400°F. Spray large rimmed baking sheet with nonstick spray.

2 Spread squash in single layer on prepared baking sheet and roast, stirring after 20 minutes, until browned and tender when pierced with knife, about 40 minutes.

3 Heat oil in large pot over medium heat; add onions and cook, stirring occasionally, until lightly browned, about 10 minutes. Add garlic and ginger; cook, stirring, until fragrant, about 1 minute. Stir in curry powder and cook 30 seconds longer. Add roasted squash, broth, coconut milk, salt, and cayenne; stir to combine. Simmer, covered, 10 minutes to allow flavors to blend. Remove from heat and let cool slightly.

4 Puree soup in batches in blender or food processor, or use immersion blender to puree in pot.

5 Reheat soup if necessary. Stir in lime juice. Ladle soup evenly into 8 bowls; garnish with scallions and cilantro.

Per serving (generous 1 cup): 170 Cal, 5 g Total Fat, 2 g Sat Fat, 365 mg Sod, 32 g Total Carb, 7 g Sugar, 5 g Fib, 3 g Prot.

cook's tip

Save time by purchasing already peeled and seeded butternut squash chunks.

Coconut-Curry
Butternut
Squash Soup

Grilled Zucchini with Lemon-Herb Feta

ZUCCHINI & YELLOW SQUASH

Grilled Zucchini with Lemon-Herb Feta

SERVES 6
GLUTEN FREE
VEGETARIAN

2 scallions, finely chopped

3 tablespoons crumbled feta

2 tablespoons finely chopped
fresh mint leaves

1 tablespoon olive oil

1 teaspoon grated lemon zest

1 teaspoon lemon juice

4 (6-ounce) zucchini,
ends trimmed

½ teaspoon kosher salt

1 Preheat grill to high or prepare hot fire.

2 Stir together scallions, feta, mint, oil, and lemon zest and juice in small serving bowl; set aside.

3 Meanwhile, cut zucchini lengthwise in half; then cut each half into 4 or 5 pieces. Put zucchini on large plate; spray with nonstick spray and sprinkle with salt, tossing to coat evenly.

4 Place zucchini on grill rack and grill, turning, until well marked and tender, about 3 minutes per side. Transfer zucchini to small serving platter and top with herbed feta.

Per serving (about 5 pieces zucchini and 1 heaping tablespoon feta mixture): 54 Cal, 4 g Total Fat, 1 g Sat Fat, 223 mg Sod, 4 g Total Carb, 3 g Sugar, 1 g Fib, 2 g Prot.

Tri-Color Vegetable Ribbons with Thyme and Pecorino

SERVES 4
GLUTEN FREE
VEGETARIAN

2 small zucchini, trimmed

2 small yellow summer squash, trimmed

4 carrots, trimmed

1 teaspoon olive oil

1 red onion, halved and thinly sliced

1 garlic clove, minced

½ teaspoon kosher salt

⅛ teaspoon black pepper

¼ cup grated pecorino Romano cheese

1½ teaspoons chopped fresh thyme

¾ teaspoon grated lemon zest

1 Pull vegetable peeler down length of each zucchini and summer squash to make "ribbons" (stop when you reach seedy center). Use same technique to make long carrot ribbons.

2 Heat oil in large deep skillet over medium-high heat. Add onion and cook, stirring, until softened, about 5 minutes. Add zucchini, summer squash, carrots, garlic, salt, and pepper; cook, tossing often, until vegetables are tender, about 3 minutes longer. Spoon vegetables onto serving platter; sprinkle with pecorino, thyme, and lemon zest.

Per serving (about 1 cup vegetables and 1 tablespoon cheese): 88 Cal, 3 g Total Fat, 1 g Sat Fat, 391 mg Sod, 13 g Total Carb, 8 g Sugar, 3 g Fib, 3 g Prot.

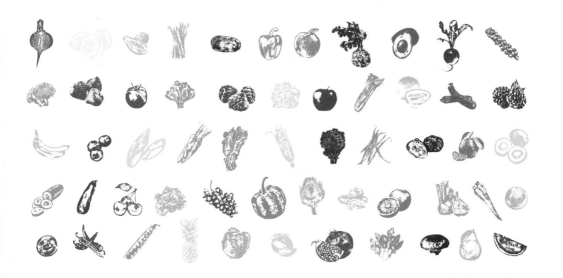

*Spiced Apple–Cherry
Phyllo Tart, page 79*

RECIPES BY SMARTPOINTS VALUE

0 SmartPoints

Braised Red Cabbage with Apples, 166
Creamy Melon and Cucumber Salad, 91
Easy Grape Granita, 104
Fresh Strawberry Salsa, 135
Mexican-Style Clementine and Jicama Salsa, 98
Quick Southern-Style Collards, 184
Summer Slaw with Jicama, 203

1 SmartPoints

Artichoke Pesto, 146
Banana-Coconut Raita, 81
Broccoli with Shallots and Lemon, 160
Buffalo-Style Stuffed Celery, 174
Carrot-Ginger Dressing, 169
Cherry Tomatoes Stuffed with Feta and Cucumber, 236
Chilled Green Gazpacho, 212
Creamy Mango Spread, 113
Creamy Thai Carrot Soup, 170
Creole-Style Stuffed Mushrooms, 214
Endive Spears with Chicken Salad and Red Grapefruit, 194
Fennel and Carrot Gratin with Pecorino, Orange, and Thyme, 197
Ginger-Mint Pineapple Salad, 126
Green Pea Dip, 221
Grilled Baby Eggplant with Yogurt Sauce, 192
Grilled Cauliflower Steaks with Homemade Pesto, 173
Honeydew-Basil Sorbet, 92
Kiwi, Orange, and Strawberry Salad, 105
Orange Salad with Mint and Orange Flower Water, 117
Raspberry-Mustard Vinaigrette, 132
Roasted Acorn Squash with Thyme, 240
Roasted Asparagus with Pepper Sauce, 150
Roasted Beet Salad, 155
Roasted Cauliflower with Parmesan, 171
Rosemary Roasted Radishes with Greens, 229
Sautéed Brussels Sprouts with Basil and Pine Nuts, 164
Sautéed Spinach with Crispy Garlic, 234
Spiced Citrus Salad, 102

Tri-Color Vegetable Ribbons with Thyme and Pecorino, 246
Watermelon Pops, 141
Watermelon Salad with Cucumber, Scallion, and Feta, 140

2 SmartPoints

Asian-Style Carrot Slaw, 168
Bacon, Egg, and Spinach Breakfast Stacks, 231
Baked Tilapia with Grapes and Olives, 103
Blackberry-Almond Cheesecake Tarts, 85
Borscht with Sour Cream, 156
Broiled Grapefruit with Mango-Honey Glaze, 101
Brussels Sprouts, Watercress, and Pear Salad with Parmesan, 163
Celery Root and Yukon Gold Mash, 176
Citrus-Basil Salad with Mixed Greens and Walnuts, 114
Coconut-Curry Butternut Squash Soup, 242
Cranberry-Jalapeño Sauce, 179
Fresh Cherry Parfaits, 95
Grilled Stone Fruit with Honey Yogurt and Pistachios, 120
Grilled Zucchini with Lemon-Herb Feta, 245
Hard-Cider Poached Pears, 124
Italian-Style Arugula Salad, 147
Mango-Cucumber Gazpacho, 112
Parmesan-Pepper Green Bean Fries, 200
Peaches with Riesling Sauce, 119
Prosciutto-Wrapped Asparagus, 151
Quick-Cook Tomato Sauce, 239
Sautéed Green Beans with Almonds, 199
Sugar-Roasted Plums with Balsamic and Rosemary, 128

3 SmartPoints

Avocado-Bean Guacamole, 154
Banana–Chocolate Chip "Ice Cream," 83
Bibb Lettuce, Cucumber, and Radish Salad, 210
Blackened Tilapia with Radish-Cucumber Salsa, 227
Blueberry-Peach Gelatin Terrine, 87
Blue Cheese and Pear Salad, 123

RECIPES BY TYPE

INDEX

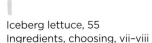

DRY & LIQUID MEASUREMENT EQUIVALENTS

If you are converting the recipes in this book to fluid ounces or to metric measurements, use the following charts as a guide.

TEASPOONS	TABLESPOONS	CUPS	FLUID OUNCES
			½ fluid ounce
3 teaspoons	1 tablespoon		
6 teaspoons	2 tablespoons	⅛ cup	1 fluid ounce
8 teaspoons	2 tablespoons plus 2 teaspoons	⅙ cup	
12 teaspoons	4 tablespoons	¼ cup	2 fluid ounces
15 teaspoons	5 tablespoons	⅓ cup minus 1 teaspoon	
16 teaspoons	5 tablespoons plus 1 teaspoon	⅓ cup	
18 teaspoons	6 tablespoons	¼ cup plus 2 tablespoons	3 fluid ounces
24 teaspoons	8 tablespoons	½ cup	4 fluid ounces
30 teaspoons	10 tablespoons	½ cup plus 2 tablespoons	5 fluid ounces
32 teaspoons	10 tablespoons plus 2 teaspoons	⅔ cup	
36 teaspoons	12 tablespoons	¾ cup	6 fluid ounces
42 teaspoons	14 tablespoons	1 cup minus 2 tablespoons	7 fluid ounces
45 teaspoons	15 tablespoons	1 cup minus 1 tablespoon	
48 teaspoons	16 tablespoons	1 cup	8 fluid ounces

VOLUME

¼ teaspoon	1	milliliter
½ teaspoon	2	milliliters
1 teaspoon	5	milliliters
1 tablespoon	15	milliliters
2 tablespoons	30	milliliters
3 tablespoons	45	milliliters
¼ cup	60	milliliters
⅓ cup	80	milliliters
½ cup	120	milliliters
⅔ cup	160	milliliters
¾ cup	175	milliliters
1 cup	240	milliliters
1 quart	950	milliliters

LENGTH

1 inch	25	millimeters
1 inch	2.5	centimeters

OVEN TEMPERATURE

250°F	120°C	400°F	200°C
275°F	140°C	425°F	220°C
300°F	150°C	450°F	230°C
325°F	160°C	475°F	250°C
350°F	180°C	500°F	260°C
375°F	190°C	525°F	270°C

WEIGHT

1 ounce	30	grams
¼ pound	120	grams
½ pound	240	grams
1 pound	480	grams

Note: Measurement of less than ⅛ teaspoon is considered a dash or a pinch. Metric volume measurements are approximate.